LEADERS OF SCHOOLS

FIRO Theory Applied to Administrators

LEADERS OF SCHOOLS

FIRO Theory Applied to Administrators

WILL SCHUTZ

University Associates, Inc.
7596 Eads Avenue
La Jolla, California 92037

CONTENTS

Appendixes

TABLES AND FIGURES

FOREWORD

As an administrator and a teacher of administration of many years of experience, I want to say this: *Leaders of Schools* may just be the most important study of institutional management in the last fifty years.

It is the only substantial and rigorously designed investigation of its kind, and it goes far beyond its specific aim of providing methods for selecting and placing administrators. The study actually provides the outlines of a theory of administrative personnel. With a combination of imagination and intellect, this work provides directions for the selection and training of institutional managers—directions that are substantially tied to a logical, theoretical system and that have a clear, pragmatic payoff for those who confront selection decisions.

I became fascinated with Will Schutz's procedures when I first heard of the ambitious study happening in California in the 1960s. He was incorporating sophisticated extensions of his already mature FIRO theory into administration and education. But Schutz went further still. He gave important consideration to sources of possible influence on FIRO patterns, such as early childhood behavior, educational values, defense mechanisms, biographical data, and cognitive styles. His energetic intellect later took his excitement about the dimensions of interpersonal behavior into another context which led soon to his highly successful and provocative volume *Joy*. Much of the groundwork for that book lay in the present study.

I am particularly pleased that the essence of this project is now about to be disseminated in the literature of institutional management, a vitally important area that deserves rigorous study and a creative union of theory and practicality.

Leaders of Schools is a seminal and timeless work.

William G. Monahan, Dean
College of Human Resources
and Education
West Virginia University

PREFACE

The history of this book begins with a research project entitled *Procedures for Identifying Persons with Potential for Public School Administrative Positions*, that Edgar L. Morphet, principal investigator, and Will Schutz, research director, submitted to the United States Office of Education through the University of California, Berkeley, in 1959. The contract for a pilot study to be completed in approximately sixteen months (Project No. 677, O. E. Contract No. SAE-8419) became effective September, 1959. The following excerpts from the proposal give some of the basic concepts of the study.

> The study is concerned with a systematic attempt to develop better procedures than are now available for identifying persons who have the potential characteristics and abilities needed to serve effectively in administrative positions in public schools . . . .
>
> The initial phases of the project involve intensive study of a small sample and will be done locally. As the research develops, we plan to expand geographically and do our most comprehensive work on educational administrators in California since they are available, and since we have the advantage of being able to keep in constant personal contact with them to help guide the development of our objective measuring instruments . . . .
>
> In brief, the primary purpose of the present study is to use the findings of the questionnaires and interviews in two communities, along with those of previous studies and the theoretical approach, to devise, try out and evaluate an initial battery of measures for assessing presently functioning administrators. It is hoped that this study will pave the way for a much needed and more comprehensive study that would include the procedures briefly explained below.

The *Procedures* pilot study proceeded satisfactorily. After approval by the school boards and superintendents involved, personnel from the following California school districts participated in this phase of the project: Chula Vista (San Diego area), Huntington Beach (Los Angeles area), and Berkeley and Laguna Salada (San Francisco area). Extensive data were obtained from 1,327 people, including school board members, superintendents, principals, other staff members, and teachers and parents in those districts. Professors Marvin Platz and William Wetherill of San Diego State College, Willard Van Dyke of Long Beach State College, and Aubrey Haan and George Hallowitz of San Francisco State College administered the test instruments and interviewed participating personnel in their respective areas. A mimeographed report (192 pages) covering the procedures and findings of this pilot project was completed early in 1961 (Schutz, 1961c).

By March, 1960, enough progress had been made on the *Procedures* pilot project to submit a supplementary proposal for the more comprehensive study to the United States Office of Education. This proposal was approved, and the new contract for the extended study was executed in August, 1960 (Project 1076, O. E. Contract No. SAE-9030).

The original research director served for the duration of the study. For the final year of the *Procedures* project, Frank Farner of the University of California, Berkeley, replaced Edgar Morphet as principal investigator.

The plan for this phase of the study was to obtain data from pertinent school personnel in a representative sample of schools and school districts in the state of California other than the four that participated in the pilot study. Fortunately, a related project (described later) facilitated the process of obtaining cooperation from most of the districts selected in the sample. Data for this phase of the study were obtained from 5,847 people in the participating districts. These data constitute the basis of this report.

For a decade before the proposal for the pilot study was developed, an organization known as the California Commission on Public School Administration had been concerned with studies and policies designed to improve the provisions and procedures for organizing and administering the public schools of the state. In 1958 the commission, comprised of representatives of major California educational organizations and institutions of higher learning, agreed that: (1) planned cooperative effort should be more significant and meaningful than isolated efforts by different groups and institutions, (2) proposals for improvements should be based on research findings rather than on customary procedures or on opinions of people concerned, and (3) considerable attention should be given to innovation as a means of improving practices in institutions and in the field.

As one important means of implementing these concepts, a proposal for a major project entitled *The Improvement of Educational Administration in California* was approved by the commission. (The commission incorporated itself as The California Committee on Public School Administration in order to be in a position to accept funds under California law and to sponsor this project.) The project proposal was submitted to the Rosenberg Foundation of San Francisco. In January, 1959, this foundation approved the proposal for the first year. Subsequently a grant was made for the second and third years, a period ending in June, 1962.

The project staff was located at the University of California, Berkeley. Edgar L. Morphet, (the principal investigator for the *Procedures* research study previously discussed) was named coordinator for the California Commission project. For the first few months before the grant for the study was actually authorized, the research director (Will Schutz) began work on the detailed plans for the research study. Thus, the two projects were closely related in many ways and each made many contributions to the other. The commission, therefore, encouraged and facilitated in many ways the basic research study and also stimulated and helped to finance a series of related studies.

In addition to supporting the central research project, the commission decided to use the funds from its grant to:

1. Sponsor work conferences to provide further opportunity for exchanging information and points of view, to facilitate research, and to upgrade programs of preparation;
2. Encourage and assist participating institutions to develop and carry out related research studies;
3. Improve the ability to use research studies and findings as a major factor in programs of preparation and in the practice of administration;
4. Get agreement on characteristics of satisfactory programs of selection and preparation and on an adequate credential program;
5. Involve practicing administrators, school board members, and college and university staff members in cooperative study and discussion of problems of mutual interest, especially those relating to the implications and implementation of research findings in improving administrative practices;
6. Get agreement on accreditation standards and procedures in relationship to programs of preparation for various aspects of educational administration.

The first work conference for representatives of participating institutions of higher learning and commission members was held in San Francisco in May, 1959, soon after the commission was incorporated and had assumed the responsibility for sponsoring the project and administering the funds. About thirty persons attended, including representatives of most accredited institutions. Most of the time was devoted to discussing problems and planning for the future.

The commission paid the expenses of one representative of each accredited college and university and encouraged others to attend at the expense of their institution or themselves. From fifty to sixty persons attended each work conference. All California institutions and the University of Nevada were represented. Six additional two-day work conferences were held, one during the fall semester and another during the spring semester of each year. The aims of the conferences were to:

1. Report developments in the various stages of the central (present) research project;
2. Plan and analyze replication studies conducted by three of the state colleges;
3. Plan and analyze related research proposals by a number of the participating institutions;
4. Assemble information on present programs of preparation and attempt to get agreement on characteristics of satisfactory programs;
5. Assemble information on selection procedures and attempt to get agreement on those considered desirable;
6. Follow developments in credential proposals and attempt to get agreement on desirable provisions;
7. Consider other issues of interest to administrators and college and university staff members.

Related research studies were carried out at California State Colleges at San Francisco, Fresno, Los Angeles, and San Fernando Valley and at the University of California at Los Angeles. These institutions submitted research proposals to, and were assisted by, the central research staff of the present project before actually beginning their projects. In addition, a conference on research design was held in the spring of 1961, at the request of representatives from institutions in the southern part of the state. Approximately fifty people participated in the conference, which was designed to contribute to the understanding of the place and use of research in educational administration. A syllabus on the fundamentals of research design (Schutz, 1961a) was distributed to all institutions to aid in designing and completing research projects and in evaluating results of the studies.

Funds were also obtained through the University of California, Berkeley, from the National Institute of Mental Health (Grant N-3473) for a project entitled *Empirical Tests of a Theory of Interpersonal Relations (FIRO)* that was closely related and contributed substantially to the study *Procedures for Identifying Persons with Potential for Public School Administrative Positions*. Since preliminary work had been done in this area under a previous grant by the research director, and since the two projects were so closely related, personnel assigned to all three studies were directed by the staff of the major research study. The grants for testing the theory of interpersonal relations provided support for three years beginning May, 1959.

In a study of this scope, the cooperation of so many people was required that it is difficult to know where to begin acknowledgments. Perhaps the biggest debt is to the 5,847 people who answered the basic questionnaire and the 1,327 who participated in the pilot study. These school board members, administrators, parents, and teachers from more than ninety school districts throughout California gave their time and energy for a goal that they had to take on faith.

Staten Webster, as the associate research director, supervised the entire data-collection phase. Janet Osborn Dallett set up the project originally and supervised the pilot study. Many research assistants contributed splendidly to various phases of the study: Nancy Watson, Rolf Kroger, Nirmal Mehra, Robert Feinbaum, Marvin Geller, Vernon Allen, William Riess, Toyo Masa-Fuse, Stella Estes, Judith Vollmar, Frank Monsanto, Frank Darknell, Ann Stockton, Ann Peck, Marilyn Salzman, Carolyn Feinberg, and James Cameron.

At several points we required consultation from specialists. William Madow assisted in the sampling problems; Frank Farner, Hollis Allen, Floyd Taylor, and Robert Clemo contributed their extensive knowledge of California education; Elmer Struening and Mendl Hoffman were very helpful in the data analysis; Eleanor Krasnow wrote the computer program for Guttman scaling that was invaluable in developing the many new scales in the project.

Members of the California Commission on Public School Administration who were central in contacting school districts and collecting data include the following faculty members:

Kenneth Lyon	University of California, Berkeley
John Ross	University of California, Berkeley
Edgar Morphet	University of California, Berkeley

Lawrence Vredevoe	University of California, Los Angeles
John Chilcott	University of California, Santa Barbara
Glen Durflinger	University of California, Santa Barbara
Rollin Garritty	University of Southern California
Richard Boyce	Stanford University
William McCann	Chico State College
John Sutthoff	Chico State College
Orley Wilcox	Fresno State College
C. K. Leonard	Humboldt State College
Robert Crossan	Long Beach State College
Willard Van Dyke	Long Beach State College
Wayne Young	Long Beach State College
Leroy Bishop	Los Angeles State College
Harold Hall	Los Angeles State College
Ralph Kloepper	Los Angeles State College
Louis Hoover	Los Angeles State College
Marvin Platz	San Diego State College
William Wetherill	San Diego State College
Wayne McIntyre	San Fernando Valley State College
Henry Gunn	San Jose State College
Aubrey Haan	San Francisco State College
George Hallowitz	San Francisco State College
Earl Miller	San Francisco State College
Frank Farner	Claremont Graduate School
Harris Taylor	Claremont Graduate School
Frederick Quinlan	Immaculate Heart College
Frank Bishop	University of Redlands
Rollin Fox	University of the Pacific

And to Charlotte Alter, who typed and edited the final manuscript and helped with the bibliography, a heartfelt thanks.

Without the generous support of the U.S. Office of Education, the National Institute of Mental Health, and the Rosenberg Foundation, the project could not have been executed. Many thanks for their confidence.

In the final stages of the project, Dr. Israel Zwerling of the Psychiatry Department of the Albert Einstein College of Medicine generously gave financial support for the completion of the data analysis. The chairman of the California Commission on Public School Administration at the onset of this project was Nolan Pulliam, superintendent of schools in Stockton. He was a key figure in developing the cooperation so vital to carrying out this study. Dr. Pulliam died during the course of the study. His inspiration and administrative facility are sorely missed; in a sense this project was possible partially as a result of his dedication and concern.

By far the largest debt is to Edgar Morphet, who conceived the original study and who was a valued partner and supporter through all phases. It was his brilliant organizational ability that was largely responsible for creating the California Commission on Public School Administration and for enlisting the cooperation of personnel from all the major educational institutions. Without that, there would have been no chance whatever of obtaining the more than ninety school districts for the study. His wisdom and advice kept the research project pragmatic and useful, and his experience helped us to find the relevant leads to follow. I hope he will be proud to add this study to the many he has inspired and nurtured in his valuable and lengthy career.

Will Schutz

Muir Beach, California
November 1976

1
design of
the study

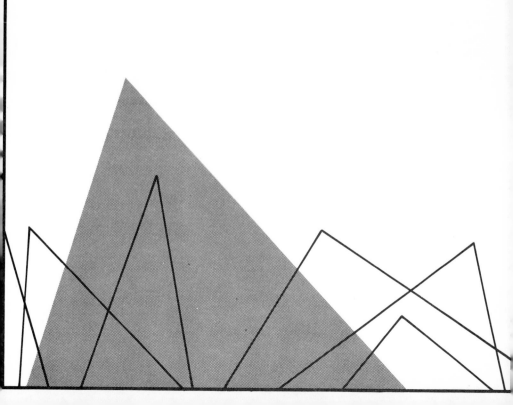

CHAPTER 1
AIMS, SCOPE, AND METHODS

NATURE OF THE PROBLEM

Administration is complex. Administrators need both personal talent and the ability to create an atmosphere in which people flourish. Their effectiveness depends on the people with whom they deal and on the type of community surrounding them. Assessment of administrative success is also complex. When can administrators be considered successful—when they hold their job? when they just keep things going? when they make significant changes? How are personal traits related to administrator performance? How do community or organizational differences influence the administrative situation? What is meant by administrative effectiveness?

To study the administrative process, the school situation was selected. By studying this specific situation in great detail, we hoped to uncover principles that apply to all administrative settings. Thus, this study is about schools and their leaders. School administrators are key elements in the question of quality education. While teachers are certainly the pivotal figures in the educational process, their efforts are sometimes limited, subverted, or nullified by poor administrators. Good administrators tend to encourage, enhance, and help release teachers' potential. In any organization, the person at the top sets the tone. When the school leader is frightened, uncertain, domineering, incompetent, or irresponsible, the teachers and the school reflect these traits. Educational upgrading requires the improvement of school administration.

The present study is concerned with understanding and predicting the behavior of school administrators, specifically superintendents and school principals (although study results can apply to other top administrators as well). No satisfactory plan for selection and placement of

1

principals and superintendents is presently available. Many administrators are selected by local districts on the basis of teaching ability; some of them are not competent administrators. Students taking work in educational administration in colleges and universities are to a great extent self-selected.

Many studies relating to the selection problem have been carried out (Campbell & Gregg, 1957; Campbell & Lipham, 1960; Dooher, 1957; Graff & Kimbrough, 1956; Halpin, 1956; Hemphill & Griffiths, 1962; Kellogg Foundation, 1956; McIntyre, 1955; Neagley, 1953). For the most part, results have been inconclusive and there is little agreement on satisfactory procedures or even on characteristics that are important for effective school administration (Hall & McIntyre, 1957). Some studies deal with sociological factors in the community (Bullock, 1959; Delwood, 1959), and others deal with behavior or with personality attributes of the administrator (Guba & Bidwell, 1957). Studies of organizations (March & Simon, 1958; Etzioni, 1961) have focused on the social system perspective of administration. Some of the work, derived from the National Training Laboratories' approach (Argyris, 1957; Blake, Mouton & Bidwell, 1962; Bennis, 1961), attempts to combine interpersonal and organizational variables to develop theory, training, and consultation methods for dealing with organizational and administrative problems. Little of the work done to date has been based on a systematic, theoretical approach to school administration, nor has any study included both psychological and community factors simultaneously.

Studies that attempt to relate personality traits to administrative success have produced little. Investigations that concentrate on sociological characteristics of the job situation led to similarly thin results. As the relevant research was surveyed, one thing became clear. If the problem of administration is to be investigated adequately, all major factors relevant to administrative success must be considered *in one study*.

The administrator's personality is certainly one variable of utmost significance to his success. Some theorists minimize the importance of this factor, asserting that the role is limited enough to allow almost everyone to perform it equally well. At the other extreme, "great man" theorists claim the role of personality is pre-eminent, with almost no regard for other circumstances.

Both approaches seem inadequate. The school administrator who is successful in an intellectual, highly educated, integrated town is not necessarily the same type of person who succeeds in a small farm community or in a remote, isolated lumber area or in a wealthy, political conservative town. Personality is apparently one of several factors relevant to administrative success.

Granted the importance of individual personality factors, which ones should be measured? Are personality factors such as dominance, gregariousness, and warmth important? Which personality theories and psychological tests should be used? Are background factors such as religion, ethnic group, and education significant? Would knowledge of the life histories of administrators shed light on their chances of administrative success? Are the major factors simply ability, intelligence, and knowledge of the job? Perhaps the values that administrators hold and the way they feel about people are crucial to success in running an organization. Clearly, some way must be found to select and measure the most relevant individual factors.

Since social climate is generally felt to influence an administrator's performance, careful measurement of the social setting in which an administrator functions is required. How can community differences be classified and measured? Should attention be given to the immediate interpersonal relationships of administrators with teachers, board members, and the staff members with whom the administrator must deal? Should the study concentrate on the organizational structure that determines an administrator's role relations to others and to the distribution of power? How important are the economic ability of the community to support schools and the willingness of people to expend funds? What of the social setting of the community—its history, social classes, ethnic and religious distribution, major industries, and attitudes toward education? Selecting and measuring these variables is another major task of this study.

The omnipresent question of all research of this type—the definition of the criterion of effectiveness—raises further complications. What is a "good" administrator? Is there one criterion of good administration or are there many? Is there an objective way of measuring effectiveness or must the assessment come from pooled subjective opinions? If opinions must be obtained, whose should they be—those of superiors, peers, subordinates, or all of these? Are administrators to be judged by their behavior or by results; are they accountable for factors apparently outside of their immediate control? Does the act of observation change administrators' behavior?

The decision was made to acquire data from three sources: (1) personality data on administrators and their interactors, (2) sociological data on school districts, and (3) criteria for administrator effectiveness.

The FIRO (Fundamental Interpersonal Relations Orientation) theory of interpersonal behavior was used as the theoretical basis for approaching the problem of school administration. In turn, this study contributed to the empirical investigation of the FIRO theory.

As the research unfolded, it became clear that new measures were required. Many new scales were developed, nearly all based on FIRO theory. These scales have proven useful for many other investigations beyond this study, since they measure areas of general interest: defense mechanisms, parent-child relations, interpersonal feelings, and educational values[1] (see Schwartz, 1976).

THE PLACE OF FIRO

The FIRO family of scales include FIRO-B, which measures *behavior* in the areas of inclusion, control, and affection; and FIRO-F, which measures *feelings* in the areas of significance, competence, and lovability. The latter feelings are assumed to underly the former behavior. With FIRO instruments, a person is scored on both the behavior he *expresses* toward others and the behavior and feelings he *wants* from others. The fundamental hypothesis of the FIRO family of scales is that every individual has the three interpersonal needs of inclusion, control, and affection and that accurate measurement of these needs gives results that enable investigators to understand better human behavior in a wide variety of interpersonal situations.

AIMS OF THE STUDY

There were three major aims of the study:

Pragmatic: devise a practical, effective method for selecting and placing school administrators and for diagnosing administrative problems.

Theoretical: expand and test the FIRO theory of interpersonal behavior and develop more scales based on the theory.

Methodological: combine psychological and sociological factors on the same subjects to study their interaction as it relates to administrative success.

Stating the pragmatic objective of the study more precisely provides a formula for organizing the study and its presentation.

Administrator A is rated R on criterion C in situation S.

A = individual administrator traits

---

[1]Derivations of these scales are presented in Appendix C. Copies of FIRO scales are available from Consulting Psychologists Press, 577 College Avenue, Palo Alto, California 94306. Administrator evaluation scales are in Appendix D.

R = measure of effectiveness

C = criterion of effectiveness

S = type of social setting

Three parts of this book deal directly with these variables. Criteria of effectiveness (C) and their measurement (R) are discussed in Part 2. Part 3 is devoted to the development and measurement of individual traits (A). Part 4 generates a classification of social settings (S).

APPLICATIONS OF THE STUDY RESULTS

If any two of the unknowns in this basic formula are determined, the following practical consequences ensue.

1. *Selection.* If the type of administrator, A, and the social situation S, are known, then the success R, of that administrator in that situation (school district) is predictable. This information has great value for school boards in the selection of superintendents or for superintendents who select principals. The method could be used to supplement other techniques. All candidates for an administrative post could be tested, the school district classified, and each candidate then given a rating indicating the probability of his success in that district.

2. *Placement.* If the type of administrator, A, is known, and success scores, R, are known, then S can be derived—the type of situation in which this administrator should be placed for maximum success. This information would be very useful for a new administrator about to seek employment and for those trying to place him. For example, it would be useful to know that an administrator with this type of personality and background would do very well in a wealthy suburban area, but very poorly in a small rural district.

3. *Diagnosis.* If the social situation, S, and the success scores, R, of an administrator are known, then a knowledge of the administrator's personal traits, A, would be very useful for diagnosis. If an administrator is not doing well in a given district, examination of his traits can be contrasted with those of administrators who do well in similar districts, in order to afford some insight into the nature of the difficulty. For example, the administrator of District T may believe that the basic purpose of education is to develop the mind of the child, but success in this type of district usually comes to those administrators who feel that education has the more humanistic aim of educating the total child. Diagnosis could lead to correction of the difficulty or to severance, depending on numerous factors, but an identification of the areas of difficulty could be aided by applying the basic formula.

In short, if the aims of this study are achieved, people engaged in the practical areas of selecting and placing school administrators and in diagnosing administrative problems will be provided with a tool to help them in their task. No matter how successful the research, these methods will be only aids, not definitive solutions. The number of variables is too vast, the limitations of the scientific method too severe, and the abilities of the investigators too imperfect to expect more. But at least this tool can decrease the areas of uncertainty.

SCOPE OF THE STUDY

Subjects for this project were selected from the public school system of the state of California. Since school districts in California vary greatly in size, geography, population density, type of school board, and many other factors, considerable stratification of the sample and the use of a large number of districts were required for the study to yield the information required. This great diversity increases the chances that results found with this population are applicable to populations in other states.

Before the sampling of the school districts, decisions had to be made to determine which administrators to study. Furthermore, since some California districts (unified) have the same school board and superintendent for both elementary and high school and some (union) have different boards and superintendents for elementary and high schools, a decision had to be made to study some or all of these. After considering available resources it was decided to study all the categories of administration represented in California. These included the following nine types of administrative situations (three for superintendents and six for principals) listed below.

Superintendents of:
1. Unified districts
2. Union high school districts
3. Elementary school districts

Principals of:
4. High schools in a unified district
5. Junior high schools in a unified district
6. Elementary schools in a unified district
7. High schools in a union high school district
8. Junior high schools in a union high school district
9. Elementary schools in an elementary school district

Since the unit of study is the individual administrator, who is part of a sample group representative of the state of California, each group of administrators was chosen randomly. In subsequent analyses, administrators were sometimes analyzed separately, sometimes combined.

To examine the interpersonal phase of the administrator's job, and to obtain several perceptions of the total situation, information was acquired from the people in the best position to observe the educational scene: school board members, superintendents, principals, administrative staff members, teachers, and parents.

DATA COLLECTION

If a school district accepted the invitation to participate in the study, it was obligated to a great deal of time and effort. A two-hour questionnaire was to be filled out by school board members, superintendent, principal, administrative staff, teachers, and parents. The planning, space, time, invitations, and so on, constituted a considerable burden on the district. In return it received nothing more tangible than the assurance that it was making some vague contribution to science and that it would receive a summary of the results when completed. Research projects requesting efforts of this type have uniformly met with an overwhelming lack of enthusiasm.

The cooperation of the California Commission on Public School Administration was crucial to the project. The Commission comprises representatives of twenty colleges and universities in the state from the Oregon border to the north (Humboldt State College) to the Mexican border to the south (San Diego State College), and all the major educational organizations in California. With this cooperation it was possible to approach each selected district from two directions. Most of the organizations publicized the study in their newsletters, meetings, and personal contacts and urged their members to cooperate. Their support helped to give the study respectability and status in the eyes of the educators. Then direct contact with the district superintendent was made, not by a stranger from a research project located at Berkeley, but by a faculty member from the local college or university representing the research project. Very often the superintendent approached was a former student of the representative and almost always was a friend of the educational institution and had considerable contact with it on other matters. The cooperation of districts was increased enormously through these personal contacts. In retrospect, it seems doubtful that more than a small fraction of the participating school districts would have been obtained without this method.

After a district agreed to participate, either a research representative or someone from the central research staff would arrange a time to administer the two-hour test battery to district personnel and a place somewhere in the district, usually at a local school building. Two teams, one for the north and one for the south, were trained by the central research staff to administer the test battery, and were dispatched to the various school districts in their respective areas.

The test battery was put into a printed test booklet.[2] Attention was given to the sequence of tests and to a written continuation between tests. The continuation explained the purpose of each test, made it self-administering, and answered questions that had arisen frequently in the pilot study. All efforts toward standardization were needed because, although all test administrators were well trained, there were many of them and the tests often had to be given under very peculiar circumstances.

The booklets were carefully checked and counted as they were returned, and errors were followed up quickly by phone or by a personal return to the district. Delinquent districts were pursued doggedly until they either returned their booklets or decided definitely not to participate. The booklets were edited and prepared for keypunching onto computer cards. (A more detailed discussion of the sample obtained is presented in Chapter 4.)

PREPARATION OF MEASURES

The same treatment was used for all three sets of variables. Content area covered by the variables was surveyed, and a theoretical framework was developed for conceptualizing the approach. Measures were selected or developed to assess variables. All measures allowed by practical considerations were administered to the population. A factor analysis was done on the resulting measures to reduce them to a more workable number.

This approach anchors the measures at both ends—theoretical and empirical. Theory without an empirical check could result in so many measures that analysis would be prohibitive. Relations among the various measures would not be known without empirical analysis. Empirical derivation without a theoretical basis leads to the often voiced criticism that one only gets out of factor analysis what is put in. A fully developed framework helps to insure that the pool of measures put into a factor analysis is reasonably comprehensive and representative of the area under investigation. To insure further that these prop-

---

[2]See Appendix D.

erties exist, the facet design method of Guttman (1950, 1954), recommended by Humphreys (1962) for this purpose, was used to describe an area of interest. This technique, also called substruction by Lazarsfeld and Barton (1951), utilizes the basic dimensions or facets of an area of inquiry to generate all possible combinations of phenomena in that area. The method of dichotomous decisions (Schutz, 1950) seemed an ideal method to use in preparation of a factor analysis.

Many new scales had to be constructed and the Guttman cumulative scaling method proved peculiarly appropriate to this type of study. This method is more demanding than the other scaling methods: it requires that scale items belong to only one dimension and that they increase in degree of intensity along that dimension. Typically, these conditions are met only if the items to be scaled cover a relatively narrow and clearly delineated area. Since the theory, facet design, and dichotomous decisions methods produced such areas, the cumulative scale was ideal for retaining this advantage.

Another virtue of the Guttman method is that, if sufficient work is done to produce a real scale, a relatively small number of items may be used to obtain good differentiation among respondents. We decided to use nine-item (ten point) scales uniformly for all measures. Ten points is sufficiently short to be convenient. Since there were so many scales to construct, a computer program was devised for Guttman scaling (Schutz & Krasnow, 1964).

Appendix C describes the total scaling procedure in detail.

DATA ANALYSIS

Measures obtained on each of the three sets of variables were analyzed in a way that would satisfy the basic formula of the study. Analysis was approached in three stages:

1. *How well are the criteria of administrator effectiveness predicted by individual predictors?* Perhaps, contrary to the major hypothesis of the study, individual measures are adequate predictors of administrative effectiveness. If there are any traits that are significantly correlated with the criterion, they would be found in this analysis.

2. *How well are the criteria of administrative effectiveness predicted by combining individual predictors?* If one variable is not adequate for prediction, perhaps a combination will be sufficient. Among other hypotheses, the "great man" theory would be tested at this stage. This type of prediction is accomplished with the aid of regression equations.

3. *How well are criteria of administrative effectiveness predicted by combining predictors and taking account of district differences?* This is the full statement of the basic formula. A major hypothesis of the study is that, from individual measures, the predictability of an administrator's effectiveness is enhanced significantly by consideration of the type of district in which the administrator works. This prediction should yield the best results and provide the data desired to satisfy the basic formula.

If the results were sufficiently promising, an instrument for the selection and placement of administrators and for the diagnosis of administrative difficulties would result. The instrument is given in Appendix A.

2

theory and criteria of administrative effectiveness

CHAPTER 2

REVIEW OF PREVIOUS STUDIES

Studies of administrative performance may be classified into the following types:

1. *Character Trait:* studies that focus on individual properties of administrators as predictors of administrative performance.
2. *Group Factors:* studies that focus on the interplay of factors present in the group situation as determinants of administrative behavior.
3. *Role Expectation:* studies concerned with internal attitudes and perceptions of both leaders and followers and with the relation of these attitudes to administrative success.
4. *Organizational Models:* studies that concentrate on forces within the total organization to gain an understanding of the actions of administrators.

CHARACTER TRAITS

After scanning the literature for a summary of leadership behavioral traits, Gibb (1954), drawing chiefly from Stogdill (1948), listed the following: physical and constitutional factors (height, weight, physique, energy, health, and appearance); intelligence; self-confidence; sociability; will (initiative, persistence, ambition); and surgency (geniality, expressiveness, originality). He emphasized, as did Stogdill and most other studies, that different leadership characteristics are needed in varied situations.

This chapter and the two following chapters appeared, with only slight changes, as one article, "The FIRO Administrator: Theory, Criteria, and Measurement of Effectiveness," *Group & Organization Studies: The International Journal for Group Facilitators,* 1976, *1* (2), 154-176, published by University Associates.

Stogdill drew up a listing of the major criteria that had been used up to 1948. Fifteen studies substantiated traits that leaders and administrators possessed in greater degree than average group members, in most cases: intelligence and scholarship, dependability in exercising responsibility, activity and social participation, and socioeconomic status. Ten studies added sociability, initiative, persistence, self-confidence, popularity, ability to adapt, and verbal facility. Stogdill then divided these characteristics into general categories: capacity, achievement, responsibility, participation, status, and situational factors.

Borg, Burr, and Sylvester (1961) combined characteristics from thirty-five different studies of educational administrators, using four functional criteria: ratings of principals by superintendent; anonymous teachers' ratings; independent observers' ratings; and principals' self-ratings. Common variables, which differed slightly for each educational criterion, were personality, administrative ability, general knowledge, professional knowledge, cooperation, tact, stimulation of co-workers, social activity, good judgment, originality, communicativeness, forcefulness, physical character, and attitude toward teachers.

Several studies have been made that used various research and questionnaire formats to choose the working criteria for their studies. At the University of Tennessee, Kimbrough (1959) devised the Tennessee Rating Guide. On the basis of the ratings of forty-eight high school principals in the area, characteristics of effective and ineffective administrators were delineated. The major criteria were good interpersonal relations; dependability; good decision making and problem solving; inclusion of others in policy formulation; intelligence; and the study of new educational techniques.

Using the guide, which had been established according to these a priori criteria, professors of administration at the University of Tennessee were asked to select three competent superintendents, who in turn used the guide to rate the least and most efficient administrators in the region. Kimbrough's a priori criteria were found satisfactory, and he notes that he found that those administrators with the proper behavioral characteristics correlated most highly with those individuals who consistently furthered their factual knowledge of the administrative field.

In the Wisconsin Studies of the Measurement and Prediction of Teacher Effectiveness, Barr et al. (1961) devised three criterion types: efficiency ratings, pupils' gains, and pre-service evaluation. The latter included: skills and attitudes, personal prerequisites, interpersonal needs, educational objectives and means of achieving these objectives, and guidance and evaluation skills. The rating based on these criteria consisted of fourteen questions about personal qualities, ten about competencies, an examination of the effects of the teacher's leadership (through standard achievement tests administered to the pupils), and a fourth area of "behavioral control"—rating of specific knowledge, generalized skills, and attitudes and ideals.

Grobman and Hines (1956) stated that effective principal behavior has a high correlation with democratic conduct. They asked eighty principals how they operated in eighty-five different school situations and then sorted the responses, distinguishing between those who operated democratically in more than half of the situations and those who did not. The responses were then reviewed by ten professors of administration from the University of Florida, who found that the most effective solution in each situation correlated highly with democratic behavior. Grobman and Hines also found that although the principals' behavior had strong effects upon teacher, student, and community attitudes toward the school, it did not affect subject matter or teacher-pupil relationships.

Several investigators have created categories of educational leadership for their own investigation. Harrell (1964) conducted an experiment in leadership behavior in a group-problem situation. Members of each five-man group were participants in an executive development program; all had taken the Stanford Management Potential Test Battery, which was used as a predictor of leadership and for assessment of the reliability of observed ratings. Two graduate students in psychology observed the behavior of each group and gave individual leadership ratings on best ideas, guidance of the group, best decisions, amount of participation, liking, and enjoyment of the group.

Platz (1960) devised a chart of the varied roles, skills and abilities, and types of knowledge necessary to an effective secondary school administrator. The major roles of the leader were shown to be in the areas of leadership, participation, management, and liaison and public relations.

Newell (1962) rated leadership criteria, in order of importance, as (1) effective leader, experienced in leadership and individual appraisal; (2) responsibility; (3) knowledge, technical and general, of the various educational disciplines. Hines (1961) presented a lengthy situation check list of desirable leadership characteristics to parents, teachers, and students concerned with one Florida school. He found the most prominent characteristics to be group leadership ability, democratic and consistent behavior, and knowledgeability. Wetzler (1955) viewed administration in terms of five roles: (1) educator, (2) administrator, (3) personnel administrator, (4) public relations administrator, and (5) business administrator.

Anderson and Davies (1956) formulated an evaluative scale for patterns of educational leadership. It consisted of the following items: (1) sees education in relation to society at large (incorporating interpersonal democratic values); (2) has a balanced view of education in the professional sense (decision making, knowledge of community and teaching matter); (3) is a specialist in the processes of administration (problem solving); (4) is a robust, healthy person; (5) has superior mental ability; and (6) is emotionally and socially mature.

Teachers evaluated their leader after a principal, Gilbert R. Weldy (1961), issued an anonymous check list to them. The criteria they found most important were (1) democratic behavior; (2) free opinion and judgment, and correction of teachers' faults; (3) clear policies; (4) frequent meetings; (5) efficient administrative organization and discipline; (6) duty delegation; and (7) community representation in policy making.

GROUP FACTORS

To describe the emergence of effective leadership, another set of investigations focused more on relations between group members and leaders than on personal traits of the leader alone.

Stogdill (1948), in some of the most comprehensive theoretical work in this area, built upon his leadership characteristics by creating the initiation-consideration rating for effective groups. It is clear from this study that the ability to show active consideration for others and initiate group interaction in that particular group situation is more important to leadership than having specific personality traits. Thus, a list of desirable behavioral characteristics is a less consistent measure of the effective leader because, in each situation, it is likely that different qualities will be most successful in mobilizing group members. The characteristic needs of each member of the group are as important in determining whether or not the group will be effective and which individual will be most successful in leading the group as are the particular characteristics that make one person the administrator or leader. The several other broad definitions of the leadership function, those defined in terms of sociometry, influence and control, and group progression or syntality, would seem to take account of the preferred personal traits of the potential and likely leader, but incorporate these into a broader structure that measures the administrator in terms of his effect upon the group.

Redl (1942), in a classic paper, reviewed Freud's definition of leader, role, and group emotions. He showed that there are constituent emotions that each member brings to the group situation and secondary emotions that are stimulated by the group. The latter contribute directly to the leadership function. The leader is the "central person" around whom the group formative processes develop. Redl defined ten basic functions that the leader can perform, such as a source of identification for group members, an object of majority emotional drives, a stimulant (ego support) for these drives, and a common conflict solver.

Many studies have developed from Barnard's (1938) distinction between "efficiency" and "effectiveness." Sharp (1962) clarified these as (1) efficiency in goal achievement and (2) effectiveness in satisfying the social and emotional needs of the group. In the informally structured group studies, more emphasis is placed on this second criterion. Group members are no longer simply tools for achieving a goal, but must be satisfied interpersonally as a part of the leader's task. Stogdill (1948) constructed two primary criteria for testing these two factors of the successful group: (1) consideration of others and (2) initiating structure in interaction. Although one criterion pertains more to task accomplishment and the other to individual need satisfaction, both are highly correlated with the successful interpersonal relationships between group and group member and between leader and group members. Stogdill and Shartle (1948) indicated in their study that, because research must be conducted within the interpersonal situation from which leadership evolves, concentration must be used primarily to find the relationships between jobs that leaders do, since "leadership is the process of getting things done." From this, selection criteria can be developed. Distinctions among various studies cannot be easily drawn. Some concentrate more on need satisfaction, others on goal satisfaction, and others on goal accomplishment of leader and group.

Halpin (1958), Taylor, Crook, and Dropkin (1961), and Campbell and Lipham (1960) have all utilized Stogdill's hypothesis in studies similar to the original one. Halpin and Winer (1957) tried to find the most influential leadership characteristics. They determined a priori dimensions and reduced these to four major functions. A number of airplane commanders rated the importance of the four variables. Their findings were that consideration was the most important trait, followed by initiating structure, production emphasis, and sensitivity (social awareness). In an Ohio State study, Halpin (1956) substantiated Stogdill's findings that the most effective leaders functioned well in both categories. Halpin also used Stogdill's Leadership Behavior Description Questionnaire (LBDQ) as a test of democratic leadership based on two criteria. Taylor, Crook, and Dropkin (1961) utilized a form of the LBDQ. They observed thirty-seven students who participated in two thirty-minute, six-man discussion groups over a period of two years.

They were joined by selected members of the faculty, who were trained in the method of the study before observation, but who judged the students independently. Each student was rated on "initiates structure" and "shows consideration." They introduced a subdivision of the first criterion, "influences structure in interaction," but this was rated far less reliably from one meeting to the second than were the basic criteria. Campbell and Lipham (1960) used Stogdill's studies of character traits such as capacity, achievement, responsibility, participation, and status and situational factors, but seemed to emphasize the initiation criterion more strongly. As the primary characteristics for effective leadership, they listed: (1) facilitating development of group goals and policies; (2) stimulating the development of appropriate programs; and (3) procuring and managing personnel and material.

Hemphill (1961) viewed administration as a problem-solving function. Through this process, according to Hemphill, the leader may take the initiative in structuring group interaction. On the other hand, Griffiths (1959) viewed decision making as a central function of the administrator. He saw the decision as closely correlated with the action itself and more goal oriented than the problem situation. Concentration on two different areas—task accomplishment and need satisfaction—is evident from these two studies.

ROLE EXPECTATION

in these studies, not only the actual function that the leader performs but the group members' perceptions of what he is doing were important. Bass (1961) stated that the leader is able to cope with the group's problems. Success depends on (1) the group members' perceptions of the situation, (2) the trainer's powers of coercion, (3) his ability to persuade others of leader value and capability, (4) his knowing when to restrict, and (5) his knowing when to be permissive.

Criswell's study (1961) was based on sociometry. She agreed that task accomplishment and satisfaction of interpersonal needs comprise group effectiveness. In establishing a pattern of leader choice, however, she alluded to Moreno's concept that the leader is chosen by "influence transmission" (Moreno, 1932). The leader, or administrator, is chosen by a large number of people or is a frequently chosen person. In the same vein, she referred to Fiedler (1958), whose many intriguing experiments led him to the view that "socio status" and "psyche status" (need satisfaction, role perception) must be found together in the most effective leader.

Hollander (1961) concentrated largely on goal accomplishment. The two most important characteristics of the leader are (1) competence in the group's central job or "task competence" and (2) active membership in the group as perceived by the other members. He hypothesized that by performing as a member of the group, the potential leader builds up "idiosyncrasy credits" and may then attempt to innovate and challenge the established patterns of the group. According to Hollander, to assume this leadership role, a person needs social perception and the ability to modify his behavior.

In another study, Hollander (1961) divided 187 cadets into eight sections and asked them to nominate three potential leaders for a hypothetical dangerous mission. He then asked each cadet to presume that he was a leader and asked which three followers each would be most likely and least likely to select from the group. This measure showed definite indications that the good leader is often selected as a good follower.

Hollander also checked his "idiosyncrasy credits" hypothesis by using a group situation. In several groups of five individuals each, the nonconformer who tried to take on leadership functions early in the sessions lost any influence he had had previously. The late nonconformer was able to challenge majority ideas, to encourage others to disagree, to talk out of turn, and so on.

Hills (1964) viewed the administrative process as mediation between institutional expectations and personality needs. Criteria of effective and efficient leadership must, therefore, include behavior relevant to the expectations of the observers. The best leadership is a compromise between the institutionally oriented and personally oriented patterns. Hills clarifies this with a diagram:

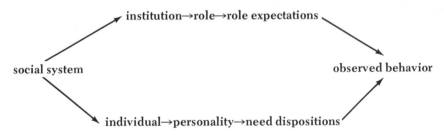

Roff (1950) had a different approach to the frames of reference rating. He used two different groups with the same rating scale. He took pilots of different ranks and had them rate each other on competence in flying, fairness, courage, administrative competence, responsibility, and likeability. Superiors rated their subordinates and vice versa. Roff found the greatest discrepancy on the interpersonal level, where superiors were rated lower than their subordinates.

Stogdill and Shartle (1948) did a study similar to Roff's. Twenty-four officers of the Naval Command Staff rated the persons with whom they worked and themselves on an RAD index (responsibility, authority, and delegation). The officers were also rated by observers on sociometric type, level in the organization, and amount of time they spent with the members of the organization whom they had rated.

ORGANIZATIONAL MODELS

Shartle (1961) said that in the interdisciplinary model of leadership, emphasis is placed on "the situation, the environment of organizations, and organizational values." He suggested that the reference points that must be considered are (1) individual behavior, (2) organizational behavior, (3) environmental events, and (4) interactions of these three. He specified certain independent and dependent variables that may be utilized to judge the administrator's performance. Major variables that may be rated on the basis of the leader alone are value patterns; situational patterns; measures of aptitude, knowledge, and skill; measures of personality and interest; measures of physical energy and capacity; past individual and organizational performance; and task or problem assigned. Measuring these variables is simple compared to measuring those dependent variables that must be analyzed as part of the organizational process, where the leader's performance is largely dependent on the group and the task situation. These variables include: decisions made, ratings of performance, measures of attitude change, objective measures of performance, tenure and mobility, work patterns, leader behavior dimensions, sociometric ratings, and learning behavior.

Argyris (1961) also concentrated on the organizational structure as the most accurate, direct route to the proper role of the leader. He said that interactors' ratings of the leader cannot be measured accurately without an awareness of a strong tendency to identify organizational controls (requirements, restrictions, budgets) with the leader personally. Each of his criteria would figure, in other words, as one of Shartle's dependent variables. They include: awareness, control, internal influence, problem solving, time perspective, external influence, and organizational objective.

Roby's (1961) concept of leadership was similar to those of Shartle and of Argyris in that he saw the executive function as the "entire process by which group actions are selected from a pool of potential actions." He did not touch on personal or behavioral characteristics, but elaborated on group action as the clue to the leadership role. Roby hypothesized that each group action is composed of "action units"; this combination of acts he labeled a "response aggregate" (RA). The group's task is to select the most valuable RA, one which is most suitable to the group's environmental state. Thus, the leader's role is to (1) bring about congruence of goals and to emphasize existing congruences, (2) propel intelligent choice of RA's and keep a broad field of potential RA's—make sure that the group becomes committed to tasks only if group members have the skill and motivations necessary, (3) focus materials on decision-making processes, (4) provide information after structure is established, (5) make final decision, and (6) function as arbitrator. Roby said that "The ability of a leader to fill any breach in the executive process may be more significant than the particular functions he performs routinely . . . the latter can almost certainly be delegated or institutionalized." The need for this function, Roby said, implies a fault in the executive structure and, though necessary, this function is probably less effective than the routinized leadership functions. He added that "truly effective personal leadership depends upon its ability to recognize when its own operation is required; it depends equally on a readiness to surrender the reins when its purpose has been accomplished." Thus, according to Roby's definition of the executive structure, personal leadership must emerge only when it is necessary to make an immediate or arbitrary decision. His view is similar to the "leader as completer" described later.

Bennis (1961), in a definitive essay on leadership theory, pointed out that organizational structure is necessary for self-assessment of administrative performance. He said, "The decision maker, then, faced with no operable means for evaluating a decision—as is often the case—and with limited data, has no other recourse than to utilize a group, both as a security operation and as a validity tester." The organization, or group in a smaller dimension, is utilized as a situational and measurement tool even when only the actual material goal is a basis for measurement of effective performance. It assumes even greater importance when the success of interpersonal relations within a group that is performing a specific task is also judged as part of the administrator's goal. Organizational theories do emphasize this group-development process in varying degrees. Bennis said that the function of authority is a combination of role and expertise and that the latter function may be further divided into knowledge of performance criteria and compatibility of human elements of administration.

CHAPTER 3
ISSUES FOR ADMINISTRATIVE EFFECTIVENESS

From the previous chapter, it is clear that there is so little convergence of viewpoints that the search for a single criterion of administrative effectiveness is fruitless. In some cases, it is important for an administrator to be an educational leader; in other circumstances the primary requisite is the ability to persuade the community to vote for school bonds; at yet other times, the administrator must be able to supervise an extensive building program. Most people are adept at some of these functions and not at others. To call any one ability "the" criterion loses a significant differentiation. It is more useful to describe and measure several criteria for administrative effectiveness and then to determine which criteria are most important for each situational requirement. The research task is to investigate the main criteria used by, or useful to, those interested in administrative selection.

RESULTS AND SUBGOALS

The goals of administration are unique in their remoteness. A scientist's goal is a specific scientific achievement, a baseball batter's goal is to get a hit, and a plumber's is to fix a sink. For these occupations the goal is accomplished primarily by the direct application of one person's skills. Not so for administrators. They must create conditions that result in a number of people functioning in such a way that an organizational goal is accomplished.

This difference leads to a special difficulty in assessing an administrator's effectiveness. A ball player either hits or not, a plumber fixes the sink or not. By and large, their success depends entirely upon themselves. But an administrator's success depends upon many factors other than his own personal talents. Industrial executives are successful if their firms show a profit; baseball managers, if their teams win; presidents, if their countries stay out of war and depression; and principals, if all their students realize their full potential year after year. The company's profit is a function of the state of the economy, the international situation, the competition, the amount of available capital, the reputation of the company's product, and so forth. The baseball team's success depends on the quality of players, the willingness of the front office to spend money for needed players or coaches, the support of the fans, and the history of baseball in the town. The achievement of the student depends on the help given him at home, his native ability, the intellectual tradition and educational level of the parents, and so forth.

The goals of education are often difficult to measure. The achievement, health, emotional stability, and happiness of each student are not easily amenable to direct assessment. To compensate for this difficulty, administrative subgoals and processes leading to educational success may be evaluated. For example, the principal's ability to motivate the community to support the schools is probably relevant to the accomplishment of ultimate educational aims. The subgoal as a measure of administrative effectiveness has the advantage of being a direct result of the administrator's actions and the disadvantage of having only an inferential relation to the ultimate goal of student performance. That is, it is not certain that schools in communities with well-motivated citizens will produce students who realize their potential, but it is assumed that this result is highly probable. Educational *results* are of greater importance, but *performance* is usually easier to measure and easier to use for assessing the administrator.

DELEGATION

The concept of leadership that best expresses the present view of administration is "the leader as completer" (Schutz, 1961b). This concept does not specify any set of behaviors as desirable for or defining of leadership. Successful leadership requires the ability to ensure that a group accomplishes its goal. Leadership functions are concerned with the total group operation and with assuring that all the specific functions necessary to accomplishing the goals of the group are being performed optimally. The role of leader or administrator requires (1) knowledge of necessary group functions, (2) sensitivity in perceiving which group functions are not being performed optimally at a given time, (3) ability to fulfill or to have someone else fulfill that need optimally, and (4) willingness to do what is necessary to satisfy these needs, even though they may be personally displeasing.

Administrators are considered effective if they recognize their own abilities and limitations and compensate for their limitations by delegating well. Delegation is one of the primary tools for accomplishing the goals of the organization (Dewey, 1922).

DIFFICULTY

Some situations are more difficult for administrators to deal with successfully than others. To evaluate administrators fairly, it is necessary to take the realities of the total situation into account. If administrators are placed in a position where it is relatively difficult to accomplish school objectives, they should receive more credit for success than if they are put into a relatively simple position. Administrative performances can be compared to what would have happened had an "average" or "the best possible" administrator been put on the job.

FRAME OF REFERENCE

The multiplicity of criteria of effectiveness was considered earlier in terms of the many functions on which administrators may be judged. In addition, each function may be perceived from several different points of view and by a variety of people (Coladarci, 1955; Hollander, 1961). A superintendent, for example, may be rated high on administrative skill by school board members and low by teachers. It is not meaningful to look for which is "really" true. All perceptions are true in the sense that they are reported as seen by some person or group. Whether or not the perception is supported by outside evidence, the perception itself is an important consideration with respect to effectiveness. If members of a community perceive an administrator as inept, they may vote against a tax increase regardless of whether the administrator is "really" inept. Perceptions are realities.

It is quite possible that two different perceptions of the administrator are both supported by objective evidence. A principal may be very submissive to the superintendent and very domineering with teachers, leading to two contradictory, but accurate, descriptions of dominance behavior by two different perceivers. Because each perceiver observes different facets of the administrator's behavior, it would not be reasonable to expect high inter-rater agreement. Similarly, principals may exhibit different behavior when they are discussing a budgetary problem with their superintendents than when they socialize with community leaders, or discipline students, or supervise teachers.

Measures of effectiveness should specify not only the area of effectiveness being considered (educational leadership, organizational ability), but also the point of view from which the evaluation was made (the person or group making the evaluation) (Halpin, 1958).

A more specific statement of an effectiveness rating takes the following form.

Administrator A is rated E, relative to the best possible performance on function C, by person (or group) P, in situation S.

The most comprehensive evaluation of an administrator's total behavior includes perceptions of all persons in a position to observe significant administrative behavior. Such persons may be called the administrator's *interactors*. Interactors of school principals include teachers, parents, superintendents, school board members, community leaders, local building employees (secretaries, custodians, gardeners), students, other principals, supervisors, and central office administrators. In most cases, these interactors have an opportunity to observe some aspect of the principal's behavior, although the opportunity is limited for many, and some members of these interactor groups (inactive parents, for example) have virtually no opportunity to observe.

There remains a serious limitation to this method of assessment. A satisfactory rating from all interactors may mean simply that the principal is performing satisfactorily. What assurance is there that the principal is doing a good job by some "objective" or "absolute" standard? Certainly it is undesirable to limit this research project to maintaining the status quo or, at best, to raising all administrators to the level of the best existing ones.

One solution to this dilemma is to add another point of reference for the ratings contemplated. The new rating would compare the performance of a given administrator with some absolute criterion of administrative excellence. This rating could probably be made best by those people most acquainted with the absolute criteria—perhaps professors of educational administration. They could rate administrators on the basis of how closely they approximate the "ideal" administrator. This would constitute a criterion that would allow a research project directed at recommending administrators who might exceed the status quo. Up to now, all administrators could, theoretically, be rated lower than the ideal, even if judged to be the best administrators available.

A second solution is to discover or devise criteria that could be agreed upon as ultimate for the determination of an able administrator. This is perhaps not so unattainable as it may seem. After considering the aims of education, it may be agreed that the sole ultimate function of an administrator is to carry out, in the most effective way possible, the objectives of education. These objectives are often stated in terms of the impact of education on the child, the community, and society as a whole. It is important for investigators to be aware of such considerations when researching administrative effectiveness.

VALUES

The decision as to which criterion of effectiveness is most relevant for a specific case is the prerogative of policymakers, not research workers. At this point, the issue of values comes up. It is up to the members of the school board selection group to decide what they want in an administrator: a good public relations person, an educational leader, someone who knows about building design, a good disciplinarian, or whatever.

The function of research is to provide reliable data from which these criteria may be obtained. If a board wants a person who will, for example, relate well to teachers, research results should provide the information necessary to maximize the probability that the board will select the person most likely to achieve this goal.

A researcher may be of additional assistance by pointing out that two of the board's criteria for its administrative candidates are in conflict. To use a hypothetical example, if the board asks for an administrator who will develop autonomous individuals among the students and who will run a sound, traditional Three-R school, a researcher can show that these two goals are generally in conflict and that, therefore, the board's requirements of the administrator are unrealistic and should be reconsidered.

If they feel that selection groups should always value a particular criterion more than others, the researchers have every right to try to influence boards to this end. However, in their role as researchers, this influence is limited to presenting evidence that if a particular criterion is used certain other desirable results occur. If they wish to go beyond such influence, they are, of course, free to do so, but they are then leaving their research role.

AIMS OF EDUCATION

As the above review indicates, the literature on administration and leadership is replete with lists of functions and different concepts of the leadership role. It is necessary to select from among the various approaches in order to provide a meaningful framework for the present considerations. The "leader as completer," as described by Schutz (1961b), uses the FIRO theory of interpersonal behavior to describe a comprehensive list of functions of a leader. This list derives from the assumption that a group has functions that must be fulfilled if it is to operate effectively and that the role of leader or administrator is to keep these functions operating effectively.

In considering the school administrator's functions, it is necessary to explore the general aims of education and the role of the school in achieving them. This provides a framework for describing the results that the administrator is expected to accomplish, assuming that all administrative efforts are aimed, ultimately, at attaining the goals of democratic public education.

The concept of education underlying the author's selection of effectiveness criteria may be outlined as follows:

1. A democracy's aim is to provide a form of government that will create conditions leading to the greatest amount of self-realization, satisfaction, and productivity for the greatest number.

2. Using the abilities of all citizens will lead to this goal most effectively.

3. Each citizen has the right to be free to determine his or her own destiny and to be self-responsible to the maximum degree possible without outside interference, short of impinging on the rights of others.

4. Public education is aimed at the accomplishment of these goals.

5. The educational system should strive to create conditions that produce citizens who realize their potential as fully as possible. All the abilities to think, to know, to do, and to create should be developed to the utmost (Counts, 1954; Dewey, 1922).

6. Schools will achieve these goals if they produce students who realize their potential in the following areas, which define more specific educational goals: academic achievement, emotional adjustment, social adjustment, and physical health.

As Wilhelm Reich (1958) expressed so well:

> The goal of democracy is to continually reduce the need for governmental or administrative interference and to steadily increase the power of self-management of social groupings by constantly removing the obstacles in the way of self-regulation. . . . To secure the peace and the freedom and the facilities to get at the "obstacles in the way" is therefore the basic task of all research and social organizations, be it in the combat of poverty, or desert, or in the overcoming of gravity.

CHAPTER 4

THE FUNCTIONING OF THE FIRO ADMINISTRATOR

MEASURES OF EFFECTIVENESS

FIRO theory provides a framework for describing administrative functioning and for integrating the empirical work previously summarized with personal experience in the areas of education, administration, and interpersonal relations. Barnard's (1938) task-oriented and personal-oriented dimensions are paralleled by the FIRO variables of control and affection. FIRO theory indicates that one other area, *inclusion*, is required to make the classification complete. Twelve variables can be derived from the dimensions of wanting or expressing the three basic variables of control, inclusion, and affection. They are shown in Table 1.

The first area of administrative functioning is the *inclusion* of all the available resources for doing the administrative job. The various people and groups that may help administer a school or school district must be identified and developed optimally by the administrator. This area is called *effective use of human resources.*

Controlling these elements in such a way as to organize and integrate their contributions most usefully is the second major area of administrative functioning, called *task effectiveness.*

Creating a personal bond among the people involved in the educational enterprise is essential for the continuation of the coordinated activity required to run a school efficiently. Ability to create these successful *affectional* relations is called *interpersonal effectiveness.*

The areas of measurement of administrative effectiveness are *use of human resources, task,* and *interpersonal.*

The closest approximation to measuring the ultimate criteria of administrative success mentioned earlier is to measure the abilities of the administrator most likely to lead to the accomplishment of the

TABLE 1.
FIRO Theory Variables

	Behavior	Feelings
Expressed Inclusion	I make efforts to include other people in my activities and to get them to include me in theirs. I try to belong, to join social groups, and to be with people as much as possible.	Other people are important to me. I have a high regard for people as people, and I am very much interested in them.
Wanted Inclusion	I want other people to include me in their activities and to invite me to belong, even if I do not make an effort to be included.	I want others to have a high regard for me as a person. I want them to consider me important and interesting.
Expressed Control	I try to exert control and influence over things. I take charge of things. I tell other people what to do.	I see other people as strong and competent. I trust and rely on their abilities.
Wanted Control	I want others to control and influence me. I want other people to tell me what to do.	I want other people to feel that I am a competent, influential person, and to respect my capabilities.
Expressed Affection	I make efforts to become close to people. I express friendly and affectionate feelings. I try to be personal and intimate.	I feel people are likeable or lovable.
Wanted Affection	I want others to express friendly and affectionate feelings toward me and to try to become close to me.	I want people to feel that I am a likeable or lovable person who is very warm and affectionate.

ultimate goals. These are the administrator's ability to use available human resources effectively, effectiveness in the task requirements of the job, and interpersonal effectiveness.

USE OF HUMAN RESOURCES

The human resources available to the schools include five major groups, each of which makes a significant contribution: (a) *community*, including parents and other citizens; they must cooperate with the school in every reasonable way that can be worked out collaboratively between school and community personnel; (b) *facilitating staff*, including administrators, business manager, custodians, secretaries, lunchroom workers, gardeners, other administrators, and nurses, must help to create an environment within which the best learning takes place, including maintaining an adequate physical plant, obtaining financial support, following administrative procedures that facilitate growth, contributing to the health of the students, etc.; (c) *school board members* must create conditions for maximal school growth (they are a special case of both community and facilitative staff); (d) *teachers* must be of the highest caliber available and teaching to the best of their ability; (c) *students* must do their best to learn up to their capacities (Campbell & Gregg, 1957).

Utilizing these resources optimally requires four steps: motivation, preparation, action, and feeling. To illustrate the operation of this process, the example of the community will be used. Parallel considerations apply to the other groups.

Motivation

The administrator must create conditions under which the community is motivated to cooperate with the schools, the staff is motivated to develop the most helpful and effective facilitating services, the school board wants to use its position to obtain the best educational program possible, teachers want to teach up to their capacities, and students are inspired to learn up to their capacities.

Preparation

Motivation alone is not sufficient, however. Once motivated, these groups must have enough preparation to know what to do and how to do it if the goals for which they are motivated are to be accomplished most effectively. Community members must be helped to understand the goals and needs of the school and to know the contribution they can make to their achievement. The staff must have access to effective methods of giving supporting services, such as maintaining the physical plant, communication procedures, accounting methods, and so on. The school board must be kept aware of important events in the school system and in education in general. Teachers must have access to the latest teaching methods and to training courses, so that they may grow in ability and experience. Students must be taught how to learn, so that they learn how to study, how to read, and so on.

Action

Even if people want to do something and know how to do it, they must have the opportunity, and the administrator must create that opportunity. The citizens must be allowed to cooperate and contribute to the schools. The staff must not be hamstrung by rigid regulations or by excessive supervision. The school board must be allowed to exercise its prerogatives in determining policy. Teachers must be allowed to teach, and distractions such as extensive extracurricular responsibilities, restrictions on teaching methods, and pressures from parents must be minimized. Students must be given the opportunity to learn, through reasonable class size, nonconstricting teaching, and a minimum of distractions.

Feeling

Finally, personnel related to the schools have the right to obtain a feeling of personal satisfaction from the schools. This is true for every social institution. Society presumably profits in the long run by educating children, but it is also important that citizens, staff, board members, teachers, and students find satisfaction from the school experience itself. If this were not desired from school institutions, society would be a place where everything is frightfully efficient but people are miserable. It is true that people will probably be more efficient when they are happy, but, in addition, it is simply an important goal of society for people to be happy (Argyris, 1957). Therefore, the administrator should create conditions that are personally gratifying to citizens, teachers, staff, and students.

The four steps required to produce optimal cooperation (motivation, preparation, action, feeling) are similar to those offered for social events (impulse, perception, manipulation, consummation) (Mead, 1938); individual functioning (Schutz, 1976a); and the action of the body (tension, charge, discharge, relaxation) (Reich, 1973). Table 2 summarizes these dimensions for all five interactor groups.

TASK EFFECTIVENESS

This section and the next one on interpersonal effectiveness involve assessment of the administrator's actual performance, rather than assessment of the result of his performance. The two major areas of performance are (1) task or problem-solving behavior and (2) interpersonal behavior. Some of the administrator's activity is directed at accomplishing the goals of the school and some at maintaining the school

TABLE 2.
Mobilization of Resources to Accomplish School Goals

Group	Goal for School	Motivation	Preparation	Action	Feeling
Community	Cooperation with school	Want to cooperate	Know how to help	Be allowed to help	School is source of personal gratification in terms of personal recognition, meaningfulness, accomplishment, and personal pleasure for all.
Facilitating Staff	Facilitation of teaching-learning activities	Want to aid teach-learn process	Know how to facilitate	Opportunity to facilitate	
School Board	Establish and maintain quality educational program	Want to facilitate goal achievement	Know how to mobilize school and community resources	Be given necessary information and support	
Teachers	Best teaching possible	Want to teach well	Know how to teach well	Conditions helpful to teaching	
Students	Best learning possible	Want to learn to capacity	Know how to learn	Be allowed to learn well	

organization through promoting successful relations among the people involved in goal accomplishment.

Administrators may be evaluated by how well they accomplish their technical and administrative goals. Within administrator's jobs there are things they must know and do that are specifically administrative.

A survey of literature on the subject revealed six major areas of administrative skills.

Decision Making: ability to make sound, well-thought-through decisions about all problems facing the administrator.

Organization: ability to use school resources optimally.

School Maintenance: ability to support and facilitate teaching-learning activities through procedures such as budget balancing, upkeep of school plant, scheduling of activities, dissemination of information, and selection of personnel.

Technical Knowledge: knowledge of school law, school finance, school building, history of education, and other subjects basic to good decision making in educational administration.

Communication: maintenance of open communications channels for the expression of opinion and feeling among school personnel.

Educational Leadership: encouragement of further training and innovation in education.

INTERPERSONAL EFFECTIVENESS

Administrators are successful interpersonally insofar as there is cooperation in accomplishing school objectives from the community, facilitating staff, school board members, teachers, and students. The focus is on what administrators do and feel in their interaction with people and on what other people do and how they feel toward administrators. The following is a list of the criterion of administrative effectiveness involving the interactors' perceptions of administrator's performance, in their roles both as administrators and as human beings.

Trait Satisfaction. The simplest approach is to ask interactors for their evaluation of the administrator on various scales that measure traits usually felt to be "good," such as competence, likeability, and understanding. Measurement could involve one scale and one score, and administrators would be assumed to be satisfactory to the degree that they score high on scales of "good" traits.

Personal Satisfaction. Since not all interactors want the same things from administrators, trait evaluation could be elaborated by comparing interactors' ratings of the administrator with what the interactors would like from the administrator. For example, how friendly the interactor feels the administrator to be may be compared with how friendly the interactor would like the administrator to be. This comparison takes account of differences in desires or requirements (sometimes inaccurately called expectations) set for administrators by different interactors. Administrators are assumed to be satisfactory to the degree that their performance meets the desires of their interactors.

Relational Satisfaction. The third approach to evaluation is based on the assumption that administrators are satisfactory not only if their behavior meets the desires of their interactors but also if their interactors feel that they (the interactors) are satisfactory to the administrators. Superintendents, for example, may be rated high on competence (trait) and be rated as high as parents want them to be on competence (personal), but parents may feel that superintendents regard them as incompetent, even stupid (relational).

Underlying relational satisfaction is the assumption that people feel positive toward a person in whose presence they express the parts of themselves they admire most. If interactors feel unaccepted by an administrator, they tend to feel rejected and inadequate and, in turn, to reject the administrator. (For a similar treatment, see "authentic relationship" in Argyris, 1957.)

MEASUREMENT

Guttman scales were constructed for each of the criteria of administrative effectiveness discussed (see Schutz,1961c, 1976a; Schutz & Krasnow, 1964). These criteria measures were filled out by 3,750 teachers for their respective principals.

The measures assessed effectiveness in the following areas.

1. Problem solving
2. Communication
3. Leadership
4. School maintenance
5. Organization
6. Use of human resources
7. Interest in teachers
8. Respect for teachers
9. Liking for teachers
10. Technical knowledge
11. Overall rating

The four factors that emerged from a factor analysis[1] were:

1. *Personal Traits:* qualities characteristic of administrators' personal performance—problem-solving ability, ability to maintain school plant, and educational leadership.

2. *Interpersonal Traits:* satisfaction administrator engenders in teachers—teachers feeling that administrator finds them important, competent, and likeable.

3. *Organizational Traits:* ability to integrate and coordinate the various elements of the school situation into an efficient operation—organizational ability, use of human resources, and communication.

4. *Technical Knowledge:* unrelated to any other abilities.

These measures were used to evaluate administrators for the purposes of selection, placement, and analysis of difficulties.

---

[1] Details of the factor analysis are available from the author, Star Route, Box 259, Muir Beach, California 94965.

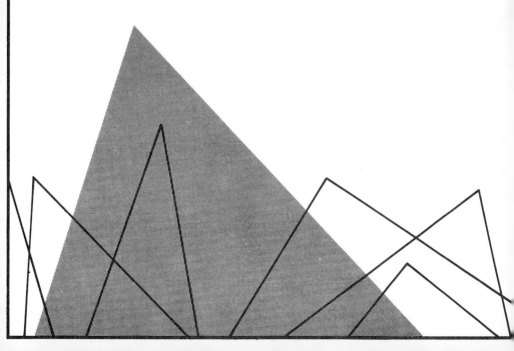

3

properties
of individuals

CHAPTER 5
SELECTION OF VARIABLES

The formulation of this study specifies three sets of variables: (1) criteria for administrative effectiveness, (2) individual characteristics of the administrator and his interactors, and (3) properties of the social situation in which the administrative situation exists. This chapter and the following chapters in Part 3 are devoted to an exposition of the selection and measurement of traits of the individuals involved in the study: administrators, board members, staff members, teachers, and parents.

Since there are an indefinitely large number of individual traits— background, physical appearance, psychological structure, hobbies, values, and so on—criteria must be established for selecting which traits are to be measured.

Four approaches were used to determine the measures most relevant to an administrator's performance.

1. *Role Analysis.* While observations of this type are necessarily subjective and somewhat arbitrary, they do serve as a good first approximation to relevant variables, especially when used in conjunction with those derived from the other approaches which follow.

2. *Past Research.* There have been many studies on leadership traits (see Gibb, 1954) and, concurrently, on the interactional characteristics of leader and follower (Haythorn, 1953; Schutz, 1955). These latter studies focus on the factors that lead to general traits such as "getting along well" with people. For example, some studies stress the importance of measuring defense mechanisms (Cohen, 1956; Waxler, 1960) and some studies consider the similarities in many background characteristics of leader and follower to be irrelevant as measures for determining leadership success.

3. *Theory*. There have been a few attempts to organize research in the study of leadership and interpersonal behavior into a theoretical framework. These theories are useful for relating various concepts that are not obviously connected. In addition, theory often points to relevant areas of investigation that may not spontaneously emerge from the more pragmatic approaches, for example, the relevance of early childhood relations with authority figures.

4. *Empirical Analysis*. The three preceding methods are for the rational selection of variables potentially relevant to the prediction of administrative success. After variables have been selected by rational methods and measures are derived, these methods may be subjected to an empirical test of their independence. Although there may be sound theoretical reasons for selecting each measure, several of them may measure virtually the same quality. Role analysis, for example, may indicate the importance of the trait of leadership in administrative success; past research may suggest that dominance is important; and theory may recommend the inclusion of initiating structure. But it is quite possible that the traits are statistically intercorrelated. The empirical techniques of factor, cluster, and latent structure analysis are frequently used to reduce a large number of variables to a more workable number without appreciable loss of predictive power.

ROLE ANALYSIS

The detailed study of the role of the administrator presented in Part 2 revealed that the administrator must be able to:

1. Deal effectively with subordinates, peers, and superiors;
2. Motivate, guide, and enable these people to function effectively;
3. Make sound decisions, that is, know how to recognize a problem, gather relevant evidence, consider alternatives and take appropriate action;
4. Acquire sufficient technical and general knowledge;
5. Know his own weaknesses and use subordinates to compensate for them;
6. Use available human resources and inspire the respect and liking of the people involved.

Social variables introduce another set of traits relevant to administrative success, the compatibility of the administrator's personal characteristics with those of the people in the social setting in which he functions. Compatibility applies to background traits, such as religion, ethnic group, and marital status, and to personal character, values about education, politics, and other public issues.

PAST RESEARCH AND THEORY

The review of the research of administrative effectiveness concluded that there was little convergence of viewpoint except possibly on the value of Barnard's (1938) initial distinction between task-oriented and interpersonal-oriented factors in administrative interaction. These variables are parallel to the FIRO dimensions of control and affection. FIRO theory suggests a third area, parallel to inclusion, namely the ability to use human resources.

FIRO THEORY APPLIED TO EDUCATIONAL ADMINISTRATION

Although it is now broader (see Schutz, 1973), FIRO theory was devised originally to account for interpersonal behavior. Since the school administration situation is largely interpersonal, the theory is particularly applicable. Following are some of the hypotheses that were derived from the theory and applied to the administrative setting.They suggest several areas of measurement of individual variables.

Hypothesis of Interpersonal Needs

1. *Every individual has three interpersonal needs: inclusion, control, and affection.*
2. *Inclusion, control, and affection constitute a sufficient set of areas of interpersonal behavior for the prediction and explanation of interpersonal phenomena.*

These statements mean that there are three important areas of interpersonal behavior which, if not considered in an investigation, will lead to a poor correlation between prediction and outcome; furthermore, the addition of any other variables beyond these three will yield an insignificant increment in predictive power.

Hypothesis of Relational Continuity

This hypothesis states the relation between interpersonal behavior in early childhood and interpersonal behavior through adulthood. The hypothesis includes:

1. *The assertion of a relation between behaviors that occur at different times of life;*
2. *The mechanisms through which relational continuity operates;*

3. *The degree to which these mechanisms are effective for different adulthood situations.*

A focus for the study of an administrator's behavior is the relation of his present behavior on the job to his behavior during earlier periods of his life. If the pattern of an administrator's interpersonal behavior can be traced back to its origins, a much better understanding of his present performance may be possible. For example, an administrator's behavior and feelings toward authority figures or toward female subordinates may be illuminated by reference to his early relations with his father or older brother in the first case and with his younger sisters in the second case.

Testing this hypothesis required measurement of the childhood relations of the administrator with his parents and similar current relations with present interactors. An elaboration of the hypothesis is presented in Chapter 8 along with a description of an appropriate measuring instrument, LIPHE (Life Interpersonal History Enquiry).

Hypothesis of Compatibility

Compatibility of an administrator and his interactor (teacher, staff, board member, parent) is positively correlated with the interactor's rating of the administrator's effectiveness.

Administrator and interactor can be studied in terms of personal, interpersonal, intellectual, and sociological factors. The relationship can be considered in terms of how similar they are to one another, and how they differ from one another or are complementary.

Compatibility with respect to defense mechanisms, educational values, cognitive style, and intelligence is measured in terms of similarity. The hypothesis states that the more similar the administrator is to each interactor on these characteristics, the higher will be the effectiveness rating the interactor gives the administrator.

In the case of interpersonal characteristics, compatibility is explored by using the formulations of the FIRO framework and taking into account both similarity and difference. FIRO theory defines the agreement between the initiator and the receiver of behavior and the atmosphere in which people prefer to interact.

Hypothesis of Compatibility Development

Compatibility of an administrator with salient others in the areas of inclusion, control, and affection, respectively, correlates positively with effectiveness during the first, second, and third phases of administrative interaction.

The compatibility hypothesis refers to an interpersonal relation at a specific point in time. The hypothesis of group development (presented in Schutz, 1958, but not used in the present study) may be integrated with the theory of compatibility to generate hypotheses about the evolution of the relation between administrator and interactor.

The hypothesis of group development asserts that the earliest preoccupations of group members are with inclusion problems—whether or not to belong to the group and how much to participate. As these issues become resolved, problems of control come into focus—who will lead and who will follow. Finally, affection problems emerge—how emotionally involved the group members will be with one another.

Applied to school administration, the combination of the hypotheses suggests that the administrator's compatibility with school and community members in the interpersonal areas of inclusion, control, and affection may influence his effectiveness, depending on how long the administrator has served in a particular school system. The hypothesis of compatibility development suggests that when the administrator is just starting out, it is most important that he be compatible with his staff and community with respect to inclusion. At some later period, control compatibility becomes important. And finally, when he is well established in a job, compatibility with respect to affection will have the most influence on administrative effectiveness.

Confirmation of this hypothesis has important implications for administrator selection. It suggests, for example, that a particular principal might be relatively ineffective in a given school system for the first year (incompatible with respect to inclusion), but later develop into an extremely effective person for the job (compatible with respect to control and affection). Or a principal might function very well in a school system for a few years (compatible with respect to inclusion and control), but later become much less effective (incompatible with respect to affection).

Hypothesis of Interpersonal Symbolism

The attitudes and ideas a person holds about educational values are positively correlated with his orientations toward interpersonal relations.

This hypothesis asserts that an individual's behavior and attitudes toward abstract ideas are predictable from a knowledge of his behavior and attitudes toward people.

In previous studies it has been found that political attitudes are significantly related to interpersonal orientations (Christiansen, 1959; Gladstone, 1955; Scott, 1960; Schutz, 1958). In the last named study, people who expressed a strong desire to be controlled by others projected these attitudes into the political sphere, agreeing, for example, that the President should make it a policy to leave problems to his subordinates until it is absolutely necessary for him to deal with the problem personally.

The same relation should hold between values toward education and interpersonal orientations. Educational values are seen as a function of the feelings and behavior one expresses toward, and wants from, people. Thus, the administrator's approach to education should be predictable from a knowledge of his approach to people.

AREAS OF INDIVIDUAL MEASUREMENT

From a consideration of these three sources of information—role analysis, past research, and theory—a classification of measures was developed, designed to cover the areas of individual measurement most likely to be related to administrative effectiveness. The following dimensions were chosen for measurement.

Present and Past

Theoretical considerations indicate the importance of exploring a person's past relationships as well as those in the present. The LIPHE[1] (Life Interpersonal History Enquiry) scales were devised to measure early childhood relations with parents; birth order, size of family, and sibling pattern were asked of each respondent. All other instruments in the study relate to the present.

Emotional and Cognitive

Many studies point to the relevance of both intellectual capacity and style and of personal and interpersonal factors. A modified form of the Concept Mastery Test (Terman, 1939) was used to measure general intellectual capacity. A new test of knowledge of educational administration was devised, and two scales of cognitive style—Imagination and Certainty—were derived from the Myers-Briggs Type Indicator (Myers, 1962).

---

[1]For the source of scales, see Appendix D.

Behavior and Feelings

Behavior is not always predictable from feelings. The FIRO-F (Fundamental Interpersonal Relations Orientation-Feelings) questionnaire measures feelings about interpersonal relations, while the COPE (Coping Operations Preference Enquiry)[2] questionnaire measures defense or coping mechanisms.

Background Traits and Values

Certain traits exist at birth and others are results of an individual's life history. Through the course of his life history an individual develops a set of values to deal with the world. Educational values especially relevant to this study were measured by a new instrument called VAL-ED.[2] In addition, political values were measured through a question about political philosophy. A person's religious preference is sometimes a combination of inheritance and choice. Background traits that a person is born with include sex, age, ethnic background, and father's education. Other characteristics acquired during life history are marital status, education, income, and mobility. The latter were obtained by single questions. In addition, there were three traits specific to administrators that were often hypothesized as relevant to administrative success. They were the number of years in the position of administrator, the number of years in full-time teaching experience, and the field of specialization during training.

---

[2]For the source of questionnaires, see Appendix D.

CHAPTER 6

DEFENSE OR COPING MECHANISMS (COPE)

In the study of human interaction, investigation of characteristic ways in which people avoid anxiety or exposure increasingly has attracted attention. Most theories of psychology assume that there are difficult and threatening aspects to everyone's personality—such things as feelings of inferiority, impulses to hostility, feelings of inadequacy, feelings of insignificance, and strong lusts and desires. Much human activity is spent in preventing others from learning about these parts that often one hides even from oneself.

DEVELOPMENT OF ANXIETY

Techniques for avoiding or distorting such feelings are often called defense or coping mechanisms and are thought by many psychologists to be necessary, to some degree, in order to maintain effective functioning. Further, some theorists feel that defenses so fully color the ways in which people present themselves to the world that they constitute the main basis for liking or disliking others.

Anxiety is present much of the time in human interchanges. Sometimes immediate situations are the source, such as when administrators appear before the school board and their competence is challenged. Sometimes anxieties are lifelong and are carried around as part of the "character armor " of a person, such as the administrator who cannot form close relations with colleagues because the anticipated pain of eventual rejection or separation is too great.

Since the overwhelming majority of administrators' time is spent interacting with people, their characteristic mode of dealing with anxiety is of central concern. Experiments have shown that certain types of coping are reacted to more favorably than others (Cohen, 1956).

Unfortunately, the theoretical and experimental literature in the field of defenses has not kept pace with the growing realization of the importance of defense mechanisms in human life. The classical work of Anna Freud (1946) was the first major advance over the seminal ideas of her father. To organize this work and the more recent investigations in this field, a theoretical framework based on the FIRO theory will be presented, and the work of other authors will be related to this framework. The theoretical development of this framework and construction of the COPE instrument was done in collaboration with Dr. Nancy Waxler and is reported in detail in her dissertation (Waxler, 1960).

The FIRO theory of interpersonal needs postulates that the basic needs of inclusion, control, and affection must be satisfied, with satisfaction meaning an optimum *expression* of a certain kind of behavior (expressed) and an optimum *receipt* of this behavior from others (wanted). According to the demands of a particular interpersonal situation, there is an ideal behavior, namely, behavior that is consistent with one's self-ideal. Anxieties arise from a discrepancy between ideal behavior or feelings and the actual behavior or feelings of the individual in the immediate situation. The unsatisfactory present behavior can be caused either by some compulsion inside the person or by some external circumstance such as being in a working situation where certain types of behavior are prohibited.

Interpersonal situations have three components:

Subject (S):   the person (ego) in whom feeling exists.

Feeling (→):   the feeling or affect directed from subject to object.

Object (O):   the target, usually a person, toward which feeling is directed.

This situation may be represented as S→O, subject has feeling toward object. Coping mechanisms operate to bring the S→O behavior or feeling into congruity with the S→O of the ideal and thus obtain an acceptable way of perceiving the self in relation to others. In order to alter or distort the basic situation, any one or more of the components of the interaction schema may be changed. This alteration or distortion is the function of a coping mechanism. It is defensive because the original feeling toward the original object is not worked through or resolved, but instead a change in the S→O schema is brought about so that, temporarily, the feeling can be handled acceptably.

Some examples will clarify this concept. Suppose the true feeling of a male subject is "I hate my father." His self-ideal says, however, "I am the kind of person who likes people." He can change any one of the three S→O components in these ways:

1. Changing the subject: "It is not I who dislike my father. Other people dislike him." (Projection)
2. Changing the feelings: "I love my father." (Reaction formation)
3. Changing the object: "It is not my father I dislike, but policemen instead." (Displacement)

All these distortions involve repression of part of the original S→O schema, which then allows a new interpretation to be substituted—one that is more acceptable to the self-ideal. This new schema also allows a temporary lowering of the anxiety level.

THE LITERATURE OF DEFENSE MECHANISMS

If the idea of discrepancy and S→O components is an accurate explication, then coping mechanisms discussed in the psychological literature should be translatable into this terminology without distorting their usual meaning and without adding characteristics that are not clinically valid. Following are the major defense mechanisms usually described in the literature.

1. *Denial.* The existence of a feeling about a certain object is disclaimed.
   Fenichel (1945): *"I don't know who this person in my dream represents, certainly not my mother."*
2. *Identification with Aggressor.* The qualities of the opponent are assumed, with a change of feeling toward the opponent.
   Airchorn (1935): *threatened by teacher, boy made same grimaces as teacher did when scolding him; boy tried to master anxiety by involuntarily imitating teacher.*
3. *Symptom Formation.* Feeling directed toward another is first repressed, then turned toward self, resulting in symptoms.
   Alexander (1948, 1952): *hostile impulses to mother-in-law repressed, and then manifested in symptoms (weakness, palpitation).*
4. *Turning Against Self.* Aggression and sadism against others are turned toward self when aggression is not acceptable and guilt feelings exist.
   A. Freud (1946): *child who hated mother turned hatred inward and tortured herself with self-accusations and feelings of inferiority.*
5. *Reaction Formation.* The opposite emotional attitude is adhered to; the object stays the same, affect is reversed.
   Fenichel (1945): *mother who unconsciously hates her child may develop an extreme affection for the child.*

6. *Rationalization.* Feeling is isolated through reasoning, in order to reinterpret behavior.
   Alexander (1948, 1952):*"I attack him because he is wrong, not because I envy him."*

7. *Isolation.* Emotional significance of object is isolated from dealings with object; or object is split.
   Fenichel (1945): *splitting of contradictory feelings toward objects—for example, the good mother vs. the wicked step-mother in fairy tales.*

8. *Undoing.* Original act is repressed with another act confirming isolation of impulses; carries isolation into behavior.
   A. Freud (1946): *case of hand-washing compulsion as an attempt to undo an unacceptable act done with the hands.*

9. *Intellectualization.* Feelings are turned into ideas that can be dealt with in isolation.
   May (1959): *fears of childbirth dealt with by discussions of pseudo-scientific nature.*

10. *Avoidance.* Avoidance of environment in which difficulty occurs.
    A. Freud (1946): *child avoids situations in which he compares unfavorably in skill (may be some kind of conscious isolation).*

11. *Projection.* One's own affect and impulse are shifted onto others.
    A. Freud (1946): A woman's hatred for female love objects was transformed into conviction that she herself was hated and persecuted.

12. *Displacement.* Transfer of feeling from one object to another.
    A. Freud (1946): *Little Hans's displacement of aggressive impulses from father to an animal.*

13. *Regression.* Object, drive, or act may change to an earlier form, as when an adult becomes "confused" and needs help when he is in an anxious situation.

Various types of alterations are apparent in these mechanisms.

Subject can be:
1. Self
2. Other

Feelings can be:
1. Not expressed
   a. denied (not dealt with)
   b. isolated (present but ignored or demeaned)

2. Expressed
   a. altered
   b. expressed without alteration

Object can be:

1. Other
2. Substitute or new other
3. Self

Definitions of terms used in these descriptions follow.

Denied: The subject disclaims the existence of the object or of the feeling toward the object; no new S→O schema is substituted for this denied one.

Isolated. The original S→O schema and the feelings are acknowledged, but the emotional connotation of the schema is separated from the cognitive meaning; thus, the S→O discrepancy is recognized, but this generated anxiety is ignored.

Altered. The content of the affect toward an object is altered; it may be reversed, partially reversed, or replaced by another feeling.

Not Altered. The content of the affect in the original S→O schema is not changed (nondefensive).

Combining the above major methods in defensiveness into one table will indicate the relationships between different types of defenses. This type of analysis has been called a substruction (Lazarsfeld & Barton, 1951) or a facet design (Guttman, 1960; Foa, 1963) and is explained more fully in Appendix C.

MEASUREMENT: COPE

The COPE (Coping Operations Preference Enquiry)[1] scale was developed to measure the relative preference of the respondent for each of several coping mechanisms.

Situations were derived to describe all the types of interpersonal anxiety possible within the framework: too much and too little inclusion, control, and affection.

There are six possible anxieties related to an individual's own behavior toward others and six related to other people's behavior toward the self. In addition, all six anxieties can occur for feelings as well as behavior. These are schematized in Table 3.

---

[1]For the source of scale, see Appendix D.

TABLE 3.
Types of Interpersonal Anxieties

		Self Toward Others		Others Toward Self	
		Behavior Level	Feeling Level	Behavior Level	Feeling Level
Too Much	Inclusion				
	Control				
	Affection				
Too Little	Inclusion				
	Control				
	Affection				

Below is a description of each cell of Table 3.

Anxieties about self-to-other behavior

> Too much:
> Inclusion—I am with people too much.
> Control—I am too dominating.
> Affection—I get too personal.

> Too little:
> Inclusion—I do not mix with people enough.
> Control—I am not decisive enough.
> Affection—I am too cool and aloof to people.

Anxieties about other-to-self behavior

> Too much:
> Inclusion—People do not leave me alone enough.

Control—People boss me around too much.
Affection—People get too personal with me.

Too little:
Inclusion—People do not pay enough attention to me.
Control—People do not help me enough.
Affection—People do not act personal enough with me.

Anxieties about self-to-other feelings

Too much:
Inclusion—I respect everyone's individuality too much.
Control—I respect everyone's competence too much.
Affection—I like people too much.

Too little:
Inclusion—I do not respect people as individuals enough.
Control—I do not trust people's abilities enough.
Affection—I do not like people enough.

Anxieties about other-to-self feelings

Too much:
Inclusion—People feel I am too important.
Control—People respect my abilities too much.
Affection—People like me too much.

Too little:
Inclusion—People do not feel that I am significant enough.
Control—People do not respect my abilities enough.
Affection—People do not like me enough.

The coping mechanisms could be explored for each anxiety. COPE explores only self-to-other behavior. A hypothetical situation is presented to evoke each anxiety and the subject must respond with defense preferences. Within each of these situations all components of the anxiety paradigm are presented to the subject.

CHAPTER 7

EDUCATIONAL VALUES (VAL-ED)

PHILOSOPHICAL BASIS

One philosophy of education may be more conducive to effective administration than another. Investigators over the past decades have focused on selecting philosophies of education and devising methods of measuring these philosophies.

Until recently, little research had been focused on the place of values in education or on the various approaches to education itself. It has often been suggested, however, that the values held by an educator influence his approach to the teaching-and-learning situation, to his students, and to educational conduct in general.

Definitions of "values" are many and relatively similar. Davis (1948) said, "A value is that which is considered desirable and which is thought worthy of being pursued." Kluckhohn (1951) stated, "A value is a conception, explicit or implicit, distinctive of an individual or characteristic of a group, of the desirable which influences the selection from available modes, means, and ends of action." Mort and Ross (1957), conforming with this general consensus and expanding upon it, said, "1) the culture has a series of definable sanctions, 2) those sanctions have reasonable bases, and when stated as principles are dimensions of goodness in action, 3) these principles can be a series of tests to decide whether or not a proposed act will be a wise action."

Weisskopf (1959) identified three approaches to values in modern thought, corresponding to the naturalist, humanist, and ontological models of man.

Naturalist. For the *naturalist*, reality is limited to the facts of the world as presented by the senses. All else, values included, are lower types of reality and require factual verification by the senses in order to be acknowledged as real. Reality is arrived at by an application of logic to observed fact. For these thinkers, society is built on a scientific procedure; socially, it is success that decides about truth value. Values are both scientific and social virtues, and are derived from the scientific process and from the rules governing a society in which the empirical scientific attitude is predominant. In other words, values are derived from life, from nature, from human existence, by observation, and, like scientific laws, they can be verified, confirmed, and validated by the observed facts. Bronowski (1959) asserted that the ultimate validation of values is survival: "A fundamental value system must fit the society which hopes to live and survive by it." He further maintained that values are an instrument of evolution. When speaking of values, Margenau (1959) distinguished the factual and the normative. He equated these to a corresponding dichotomy in the field of science: the descriptive and the theoretical. Factual values are "observable preferences, appraisals, and desires of concrete people . . . are neither right nor wrong but are facts of observation." "Normative values are the ratings . . . which people ought to give to value objects." In short, values are norms. "A factual or logical statement interconnects two data in the form of an 'is'; values and norms interconnect data in the form of an 'ought to' or 'ought not to'" (Weisskopf, 1959). Much controversy has been aroused by this philosophy, and it remains in the main current of modern thought.

   Humanist. The *humanist* approach to values is based on a holistic method of acquiring knowledge. It considers the totality of human experience—including sensorial facts, inner experience, imagination, fantasy, and thought—to establish knowledge, logic, factual observation, empathy, and intuition. Humanist thinkers share with the naturalists the belief that values are, in some way, derived from life, from nature, from human existence. But they differ from naturalists in the way they view the human situation. Their point of view resembles that of the ontologists because they include elements of transcendence in their image of human existence. The main difference between naturalists and humanists is that in the human self the humanists have found a unifying principle (Bronowski, 1959). Allport (1961), Fromm (1947), Goldstein (1940), Maslow (1959), and Sorokin (1937) all adhere to humanistic philosophy. They hold that the ultimate values are love, creativeness, and participation without impairment of individuation. The person is the unity within which facts and values are united. Both the humanists and the naturalists have the same premise: values can be confirmed by reality. They differ in the definition of reality. The naturalists include only the nonhuman reality, or where they do include human reality, "they include only those aspects of it which are isomorphic with the reality of nature, the finite, the conditioned, the realm of necessity" (Weisskopf, 1959). Human reality for humanists includes "those aspects which cannot be subsumed under the finite, the conditioned, the necessary, such as memory, imagination, fantasy, consciousness, self-awareness, and reason and the human ability to transcend the given, conditioned, finite situation" (Weisskopf, 1959). Although naturalists see facts and values as separate and often as opposites, these are viewed by humanists as unified in the human being. Self-actualization, when seen in this light, means the existential realization of a unity that is potentially pre-existent in the human person. It implies balance and integration and points to the union of opposites: the essence of ultimate values. This alone is the ultimate value for humanists, and it can be accomplished by the unifying effects of love.

Ontological. The *ontological* image goes one step further; it seeks to transcend the facts of sensory observation and of intuitive experience (Tillich, 1959, and Suzuki, 1957). Ontologists say, "Values are derived from the essential structure of being." They reject at the outset the naturalistic separation between the world we encounter and the realm of values. Values are thought of as autonomous because they are rooted in the human's essential being. They have a command and imperative character because "the moral law is man's essential nature appearing as commanding authority" (Tillich, 1959). The imperative nature of values stems from the estranged state of existence in which man finds himself because of the existential split between essence and existence. Ultimately, the ontologists say, values are part of reality, of being; only through existential distortion are they made to appear as separated. Likewise, ultimate "unity is seen in being itself, in that realm, in that sphere in which all estrangement is dissolved, in which essence and existence, fact and value, being and potentiality are united and harmonized" (Weisskopf, 1959).

Weisskopf, in trying to sum up the similarities and differences between those approaches, states, ". . . the naturalists move on the level of the antinomies; the humanists stress the polarity of the antinomies and their unity on a purely human level; and the ontologists attribute a higher reality value to the dimension of unity. They all strive for unity through love but within different dimensions."

TWO MAJOR APPROACHES TO EDUCATIONAL VALUES

In studies of educational values two major approaches have emerged. Willower (1961) described these as (1) the descriptive analysis of values, with the major focus on discovering the actual effect of social and individual values in the administrative process, and (2) the normative approach, the philosophical treatment of values as ideals.

Descriptive

Primarily methodological concerns fall under the *descriptive* approach. The questions that are asked cover four general categories. These categories and some representative results help to clarify the boundaries of the problem of value measurement. They constitute a more detailed statement of the investigators' hypothesis of compatibility.

1. *How does the position an individual holds in an organization influence his values? Do teachers, principals, and chief school administrators differ as groups in terms of value orientation?*

Prince (1957), studying individual values and administrative effectiveness, found that there is a relationship between the extent of agreement in values held by principals, teachers, and students, and the degree of effectiveness, satisfaction, and confidence in leadership found in the school.

2. *How does the degree of congruence of values held by the various members of an organization affect factors such as morale and productivity?*

McKenna (1960) found that there was low tension in chairman-professor interpersonal relations when the chairman's view of organizational power structure was similar to that of his professors. Along similar lines, Prince (1957) found that a teacher's behavior is more apt to be perceived as effective by students whose value orientations are similar to his than by students whose value patterns differ from his. The degree of congruence in values between teachers and principals is directly related to the teachers' confidence in leadership and to the teachers' rating of the principal's effectiveness. McKenna found no significant relationship between value differences and teacher satisfaction or between value differences and the principal's rating of teacher effectiveness.

3. *How do values influence administrative decisions? Is it predictable that a superintendent of schools with a certain type of value orientation will make certain kinds of decisions?*

Everett (1961), Miller (1959), Newsome & Gentry (1962), and Britton (1959) asked these questions and found that decision making is based largely on the values one holds and that a knowledge of value orientation can indicate leadership (including decision making) style. Simon (1955) summed up these findings by saying that "administrative theory must be concerned with the limits of rationality" because, given the same alternatives, values, and knowledge, two people can rationally reach only the same decision.

4. *What is the relationship between personal values and the values of an organization? How do members of a profession learn the values of the professional group? How do personal values influence selection and entry into a professional group? How does the relationship between personal and organizational values influence conflict, satisfaction, and placement of loyalties in an organizational setting?*

This is especially important in any attempt to study administrative effectiveness. If internal conflict occurs within an organization, effectiveness will be at a minimum. If similar value orientations of the participants contribute to harmony and ultimate effectiveness, then this is an area for concern. Both Prince (1957) and Getzels (1958) dealt with these problems and found, as did Merton (1940), Levinson (1959), and Blau, Gustad, Jessor, Parnes, and Wilcock (1956), that value orientations are related to the choice of role and occupation and that harmony prevails when individuals are matched well to their occupational roles and to each other.

Normative

Willower's second approach, the normative, asked the following kinds of questions in its concern with educational philosophy.

1. *What is the "good" school? What should be the ends of education?*

Of primary importance in this type of inquiry were Dewey (1922), Mann (1840), Barnard (1938), James (1890), and Curti (1959). All these men held that the aim of education should be to prepare the child to function effectively within a democratic society and that schooling should be broad, comprehensive, and dispensed equally to produce citizens who can knowledgeably participate in their own government. They emphasized that learning by rote would not produce minds capable of free and intelligent thought, and suggested that the schools be adapted to the child rather than vice versa.

Subsequently, Dahlke (1962), Wirth (1961), and Gordon (1962) dealt with these important questions. They emphasized that the aims of education should be centered around producing Maslow's self-actualized or self-actualizing person. Gordon summed this up by saying that teachers must encourage children to value openness to experience, flexibility, objectivity, complexity, perfection, spontaneity, rationality, integrity, autonomy, responsibility, and charity.

2. *What is the "good" society and what should be its relation to the agency concerned with education? What are the implications for education of the values underlying a democratic society?*

Questions such as these also take school-community relations into account. The prevailing opinion among educators is that schools are entrusted with the task of transmitting to children those values that society deems essential. The school is therefore responsible to the community in which it functions and to society at large. Since ours is a democratic system that operates via a bureaucracy, schools must be able to teach, in fact and theory, this basic tenet.

Discussions of these ideas can be found in Cook (1957), Stiles (1957), and Gardner & Moore (1952).

3. *In what ways do different systematic philosophies imply different kinds of educational philosophies?*

4. *What are the specific behavioral implications of a philosophy of education for the educational administrator? What difference for administrative behavior should the acceptance or rejection of a particular philosophy of education make?*

The Southern States CPEA Center (1955) at George Peabody College (under Orin Graff) dealt with these intrinsically similar problems in its approach (called "competency concept") to educational administration. It noted that, frequently, the designation of a task and the method of performing it depended on a person's value base, which, in turn, was actually a theory of educational administration.

The competency concept consists of three elements: job, theory, and know-how. The job is the critical task (there are eight critical task areas); the theory is the method of performing the critical task; and the know-how consists of the beliefs, skills, and knowledge needed to perform the task.

SYNTHESIS

From a consideration of the major philosophical approaches to values, the specific issues concerning educational values, the role of education and the primary objectives of the schools, the area of educational values may be delimited and measured.

1. *Is it the mind of the student that should be the school's focus, or should the student be developed as a total human being?*
2. *What is a "good" school in a democratic society?*
3. *What should be the relation of the teacher to the student?*
4. *What are the effective relations among administrator, community, teacher, and student?*

5. *How should issues such as academic freedom and fraterniza-
tion of school personnel with the community be handled?*
6. *Who should run the schools?*

These areas concretize the various philosophical issues in terms of
specific behaviors. If a statement of these behaviors is presented in a
normative ("ought") form, the resulting measure should meet the
needs of this study.

MEASUREMENT: VAL-ED

As with the other new measuring instruments, a facet design was
developed first to provide a basis for generating the population of items
to be included in the instrument (see Appendix C). The basic elements
follow.

People. Those involved in the educational enterprise: students,
teachers, administrators, and community members.

Direction. Direction of the relationship between actor and target;
for example, teacher (actor) behavior toward administrator (target),
or administrator (actor) behavior toward teacher (target).

Content. FIRO theory was used to develop the facet of content of
interaction among educational figures. Most of the issues mentioned in the literature survey emerged when the theory was
applied to educational actors. For example, the relation of administrator to teacher in the control area covers many of the issues of
academic freedom; the relation of community to administrator in
the inclusion area is relevant to the issue of school and society. The
facet of areas of interaction is inclusion, control, and affection. The
resulting scales constitute the VAL-ED.

VAL-ED (Educational Values) Scales

Fourteen scales were administered to all respondents.
Sc = school, S = student, T = teacher, A = administrator,
C = community

SCALE NAME	SHORT TITLE
Education has intrinsic value beyond occupational advantages.	*Importance*
School should concern itself primarily with developing mind of student rather than with developing whole personality.	*Mind*

VAL-ED (Educational Values) Scales

SCALE NAME	SHORT TITLE	
*School should help student realize and use own abilities and judgment most effectively.	*ScS:*	*Control*
Teacher should regulate completely classroom lessons and activities.	*TS:*	*Control*
Teacher should be personally friendly and warm toward students.	*TS:*	*Affection*
Administrator should take account of teachers' opinions when making school policy.	*AT:*	*Inclusion*
Administrator should control activities of teachers, both in classroom and in community.	*AT:*	*Control*
Administrator should be personally close with teachers and should express feelings openly.	*AT:*	*Affection*
Teachers should participate in community activities and should be encouraged to do so by community members.	*TC:*	*Inclusion*
Teachers should conform to the dominant values of community.	*TC:*	*Control*
Teachers and people in the community should be personally friendly with each other.	*TC:*	*Affection*
*Administrators and people in the community should be involved jointly in school and community affairs.	*AC:*	*Inclusion*
Desires of the community should determine school policy.	*AC:*	*Control*
Administrators and people in the community should be personally friendly with each other.	*AC:*	*Affection*

---

*These two scales did not prove useful in this study and are not included in the 1976 revision of VAL-ED.

CHAPTER 8

PARENTAL ATTITUDES (LIPHE)

An important focus for the study of an administrator's behavior is the relation of his present behavior on the job to his behavior during earlier periods of his life. If the pattern of an administrator's interpersonal behavior is traced back to its origins, it may yield a much better understanding of his present performance. This is especially true of his interpersonal relations. A description of the theoretical basis for measuring childhood interpersonal relations will clarify the requirements of a questionnaire for this area.

ORIGINS OF ADMINISTRATIVE BEHAVIOR

Where and when does an individual learn the behavior and feeling patterns toward the individuals with whom he interacts—superiors, subordinates, men, women, colleagues? Much psychological theory is in agreement that the basic behavior patterns are largely determined in the early years of life, probably about the first six years.

How do children know what to do in the variety of situations that confront them, especially when these situations are more complex than simple physiological reactions? The behavior repertoire comes from three sources.

1. Instinctive behavior: unlearned reactions to internal and external stimulation.
2. Proscriptions, usually from parents, including:
   a. direct parental demands for certain types of behavior;
   b. parents' desires for their child's behavior, as perceived by the child.

3. The child's observation and perception of the child's own behavior and that of others, including:
   a. the child's own behavior and feelings, such as delight when
      mother gives the child undivided attention;
   b. other people's behavior and feelings, such as the experience
      of father's punishment;
   c. others behaving and feeling toward each other, such as the
      child's mother and father fighting and then making up.

The concern of the present study is with the relation between the
behavior observed by an individual as a child and his adult behavior as
an administrator.

Hypotheses of Relational Continuity

*Hypothesis I. There is a positive correlation between behavior and
feelings in the childhood situation and in the appropriate adulthood
situation in the interpersonal areas of inclusion, control, and affection.*

*Hypothesis II. The similarity between childhood and adulthood situ-
ations is greatest when sex and status similarity between the two
situations is greatest and diminishes as similarity decreases.*

The elements of the childhood situation are the child (*ego*, E) who
observes the behavior or feelings of an individual (the *actor*, A) toward
another person (the *target* of the behavior, T).

The basic relational continuity situation can be shown as
$(A_1RT_1) \underset{p}{\rightarrow} (A_9RT_9)$ in which:

A = actor
R = relates (behaves or feels) in mode R
T = target
→ = implies with probability$_p$

and subscripts 1 through 9 indicate time periods of early childhood to
adulthood.

Mechanisms of Relational Continuity

Thus far the hypotheses only assert a continuity between childhood
and adult behavior. They do not specify the mechanisms through which
this continuity occurs. These are transference, identification, and elicitation.

TRANSFERENCE

Ego relates ("relates" shall be used to mean behaves/feels) to a target in childhood and relates similarly to a target in adulthood. For example, a boy who feels exploited and manipulated by his father, feels exploited and manipulated by his principal and by his superintendent when he becomes a teacher.

This formulation is comparable to the concept of transference as presented by the Freudians and neo-Freudians. However, modern writers find that transference occurs in all interpersonal relations, not just those between psychoanalyst and patient, and it is frequently characteristic of interpersonal ties in group relations. Transferences also appear in hypnotic treatment, in mass phenomena, and in everyday life.

Everyday life is full of transference situations. Generally speaking, people interpret current experiences in terms of earlier ones (Scheidlinger, 1957).

Few empirical studies have been done in this area. Elder (1963) found that children who were brought up by autocratic parents who did not allow their child to express his views on subjects regarding his behavior nor to regulate his own behavior developed into adolescents who unconditionally surrendered their own interests and obeyed without understanding, as they had done as children. And Cox (1962) also found signs of transference from home to peer groups in that reputed aggression was high for those boys who rejected one or both parent figures.

In *perceptual* transference, actor and target are observed by ego during childhood, and ego observes the same relation in adulthood. For example, when Walter was a boy, his father tended to ignore Walter's younger sister and behave as though she was unimportant. Now Walter is a teacher who perceives his principal as tending to ignore female teachers and regard them as insignificant. This mechanism essentially states that given an adult relation, a person will tend to see that relation, in part, in terms of his previous experience with such relations. This is a transference of perception rather than behavior and feelings, which were transferred in the previous situation.

Although it appears quite interesting, this mechanism will not be dealt with in the present study.

IDENTIFICATION

Ego is related to by an actor in childhood and relates similarly to a target in adulthood. For example, a father acts in an authoritarian manner toward his son, and the son, when he becomes a superintendent, acts in an authoritarian manner toward his principals.

The psychoanalytic sense of the term identification generally implies that a child gives emotional allegiance to one parent and tries to duplicate ideals, attitudes, and behavior (Stoke, 1950).

Instead of learning through trial and error, the growing child takes over behavior patterns and attitudes from adults (Alexander & Ross, 1952) and parental dictates become internalized. The child "becomes" the parent.

The process typically is unconscious; the person is not aware that he is patterning his behavior after that of another person (Symonds, 1946).

Bronfenbrenner (1961) divided prominent theories of identification into three types that define it as: (1) a defense by emulation against an aggressor, such as a victim who is dependent on an aggressor, cannot escape his influence, and models himself after him; (2) a response to an absent or depriving loved person by seeking to replace the person through one's own behavior; for example, when a son wants his mother's nurturing responses and imitates her affectionate attitudes and gestures to secure at least partial gratification; (3) a response to a parent who is a loved and prestigeful person and whom the child is rewarded for emulating.

The present explication of the term is consistent with the narrower psychoanalytic notion in that it makes no commitment to the causes or consciousness of the mechanism as does the psychoanalytic concept. It is more specific in asserting that identification takes place within an interpersonal relation and in the areas of inclusion, control, and affection.

In *impact* identification, ego has participated in the childhood interaction, that is, the child *is* T1. For example, a daughter who was strongly disciplined by her father, identifies with her father and when functioning as a principal she is a strong disciplinarian of her male teachers.

Maccoby & Rau (1962) said that the child's motives to learn this behavior are (1) to reproduce in fantasy events that have been reinforcing (even if it is the parents who are rewarded and not the child); (2) because he experiences a high degree of parental control; and (3) to obtain vicarious satisfaction by pretending to be a person who is enjoying rewards that are actually denied him.

In vicarious identification, ego has observed two other people in interaction and has identified with the actor. For example, having identified with his father's treatment of his sister, Walter, as an adult principal, behaves toward his female teachers as his father did toward his sister.

This mechanism was demonstrated in a study by Bandura, et al. (1963) in which they found that children readily imitated behavior exhibited by an adult model and generalized this behavior to others. The results of this study indicated that observation of cues provided by the behavior of others is one effective means of eliciting certain forms of behavior for which the original probability is very low (aggression). Subjects given an opportunity to observe aggressive models later reproduced a great deal of aggressive behavior. The fact that the subjects expressed their aggression in ways that clearly resembled the novel patterns expressed by the actors provides evidence for the occurrence of vicarious learning. Subjects exposed to the quiet models were more inhibited and unresponsive than subjects who had been exposed to the aggressive conditions. Mere observation of aggression, regardless of the quality of the model-subject relationship, was a sufficient condition for producing imitative aggression.

ELICITATION

In childhood, the individual's ego is related to in a certain way by others, and tends to elicit the same relation from others when the person is an adult. For example, Kenneth's older brother makes fun of his competence and does not take him seriously. When Kenneth becomes a principal, his superiors also treat him this way. There is continuity in the type of behavior he elicits from other people.

The concept of elicitation is similar to Leary's (1957) notions of "provoking" behavior, or "training" others to respond in certain ways. Leary says that interpersonal behavior, more than any other factor, determines one's reception from others. Reflexes develop that train others, and oneself, to accept a particular sort of person, to be treated in a particular sort of way. While Leary does not go into a relational continuity concept directly, his view may be reconciled with the notion that the behavior a person provides in adulthood can be very similar to that which he provoked in childhood.

The elicitation hypothesis has particular significance for selection of educational administrators, since, if confirmed, it would permit prediction of the type of behavior that candidates will elicit from those around them.

In *vicarious* elicitation, ego identifies with the target and later elicits the same behavior as does the target. For example, as a boy, James saw his father as the recipient of abuse from his mother, and as superintendent, James gets into the position of eliciting abuse from school board members, community leaders, and parents. As with other vicarious situations, the mechanism operates by virtue of an observation in childhood of a two-person relation not involving ego.

MEASUREMENT: LIPHE

The questionnaire designed particularly for testing childhood parental relations is called the *Life InterPersonal History Enquiry*, or LIPHE (pronounced *life*). One problem in any investigation of this type concerns the validity of measurements of early childhood events. LIPHE measures these events by asking for an adult respondent's recollection. The use of this retrospective method warrants further discussion.

Drawbacks in Obtaining Data

There are many problems connected with obtaining data about events that occurred many years ago. Distortions enter and affect the accuracy of recall of persons involved in the original situation. On the other hand, observations made at the time of the original situation may not have included elements that eventually prove most significant, such as unconscious factors. As a basis for exploring the advantages and disadvantages of various techniques of data collection about past events, different types of available observations will be explored.

There are three major points of reference from which childhood events may be viewed: (1) the parents' perceptions of the parent-child relationship, (2) the child's perception, and (3) the "objective" situation (that is, the perception of trained observers). Furthermore, there are three main time points at which the observations may be made: (1) at the time of the childhood behavior (concurrent), (2) immediately following the event, and (3) some time much later, for example, when the child reaches adulthood. Each of the six variables can affect the degree of distortion that enters a recollection.

Assessment of the relative importance of these drawbacks is very difficult. However, considerations of feasibility enter. For example, the only possible direct observation of childhood would have to have been made when the adult was a child. It seems clear that only retrospective instruments (those that ask an adult to recall the past) are immediately practical. Thus, the choice made in the present study was to select a retrospective questionnaire for immediate use, cognizant of all of the possibilities for distortion.

The questionnaire must provide for a measure of relations between all childhood actors and targets, and between ego and all adulthood actors and targets. In addition, for all of these relations there must be a measure of inclusion, control, and affection at both the behavior and feeling levels.

Facet Design for LIPHE

As in all the original instruments developed for this project, a facet design of the universe of content was developed and items for a questionnaire generated from that design. The facets of interest for the LIPHE questionnaire follow.

1. *Content of interaction:* the specific interpersonal areas in which interaction occurs, inclusion, control, and affection.
2. *Level of interaction:* behavior and feelings. The unaware (unconscious) level is also a possibility but will not be dealt with here.
3. *Direction of interaction:* interaction can originate either from respondent to interactor or from interactor to respondent. Since the primary interest is the satisfaction of the respondent with his childhood interaction, these directions were combined in the item style. Each item indicates the degree of satisfaction with the childhood relation. One scale was used to discern the respondent's perception of the parents' satisfaction with the respondent.
4. *Target:* for the present study, the concentration is on the major figures of early childhood—Father and Mother.

TABLE 4.
Facet Design for Parental Attitudes

	Level	Content		
		Inclusion	Control	Affection
Father	Behavior Level			
	Feelings Level			
Mother	Behavior Level			
	Feelings Level			

The twelve resulting scales are described below.

LIPHE (Life Interpersonal History Enquiry) Scales
Twelve Scales were administered to all respondents. There were separate scales for mother and father.

SCALE NAME	SHORT TITLE
First ten scales (five examples follow) begin with: *When I was a child, I wanted my father (mother) to*	*Inclusion Behavior*
spend more time with me and give me more attention.	
allow me more freedom and to allow me to think more for myself.	*Control Behavior*
be more interested in me and to feel more strongly that I was a significant person.	*Inclusion Feelings*
have more respect for my ability to think and to do things well.	*Control Feelings*
show and feel more love and affection for me.	*Affection*
An example of the next scales is: *When I was a child, my father (mother) wanted me to*	*Approval*
be a better person.	

CHAPTER 9
OTHER TRAITS TO MEASURE

INTERPERSONAL FEELINGS (FIRO-F)

Administrators spend the overwhelming majority of their time interacting with people—students, teachers, board members, parents. The particular orientations they have toward interpersonal behavior should have a significant influence on their administrative effectiveness.

FIRO theory deals with the levels of behavior and feelings. Both levels are of importance for an assessment of interpersonal relations, behavior dealing with the action occurring between people, and feelings referring to internal phenomena known primarily to the self.

The limitation of time for administering the test battery required that a selection be made among the measures of behavior and feelings. Preliminary work with the measure of FIRO-F (for feelings) indicated that it might prove to be a valuable instrument, so it was selected for inclusion in the battery.

Measurement: FIRO-F

FIRO-F measures the feeling level of inclusion, control, and affection. At this feeling level these dimensions become significance, competence, and lovability. FIRO-F measures these dimensions in both the expressed and wanted modality and consequently consists of 6 scales. A more extensive discussion of the theoretical basis is given in *The Interpersonal Underworld* (Schutz, 1966).

FIRO-F (Fundamental Interpersonal Relations Orientation— Feelings) Scales

Six scales were administered to all respondents.

SCALE NAME	SHORT TITLE
I am interested in people and I think they are important and significant.	*Expressed Inclusion*
I want people to be interested in me, to pay attention to me, to feel I am important.	*Wanted Inclusion*
I trust and respect other people's competence and abilities.	*Expressed Control*
I want people to respect and trust my competence and abilities.	*Wanted Control*
I like people and I feel close and warm toward them.	*Expressed Affection*
I want people to like me and to feel close and personal toward me.	*Wanted Affection*

FAMILY PATTERN

Interest in the effect of birth order on subsequent functioning was given a strong impetus by the publication of Schacter's *The Psychology of Affiliation* (1959). Several studies have determined special characteristics of first-born children compared to later born, including: higher achievement (Sampson, 1962); higher conformity (Sampson, 1961, Capra & Dittes, 1962); more dependence (Haeberle, 1959); higher verbal ability (Koch, 1954); less aggression (Sears, 1951, Mussen & Conger, 1956); and less leadership ability (Roberts, 1938). Even more directly related to the administrative role is Stewart's (1961) study showing the preponderance of first- and third-born presidents.

The pilot study of the present project suggested the possibility that first-born sons tend to go—or be pushed—into technical fields, while later born sons tend more to administrative positions. Large families require administration much more than small families. Division of labor, allocation of rewards and punishment, sharing, and all the other problems of group life must be dealt with in large families, whereas they exist only in rudimentary form in small families. Not only birth order but family size might be significant in determining administrative propensity.

The sex pattern of a family seems relevant also. If a second-born son has an older sister, his family role and probably his attitude toward women may be quite different than if he has an older brother. Or if he is the only boy in a large family, he is probably expected to perform differently than in a family of all boys.

Measurement: Family Pattern

The available information should be sufficient to determine birth order, family size, and sibling pattern. This information was obtained by asking the following questions.

For each brother you have (or had) write down the number of the item indicating how much older or younger he is than you are (Check here if you have no brothers _____).

Brother #1_____ #2_____ #3_____ #4_____ #5_____

1. 15 or more years older	9. 1 year younger
2. 10 to 15 years older	10. 2 years younger
3. 5 to 9 years older	11. 3 years younger
4. 4 years older	12. 4 years younger
5. 3 years older	13. 5 to 9 years younger
6. 2 years older	14. 10 to 15 years younger
7. 1 year older	15. 15 or more years younger
8. same age	

For each sister you have (or had) write down the number of the item indicating how much older or younger she is than you are (Check here if you have no sisters _____).

Sister #1_____ #2_____ #3_____ #4_____ #5_____

1. 15 or more years older	9. 1 year younger
2. 10 to 15 years older	10. 2 years younger
3. 5 to 9 years older	11. 3 years younger
4. 4 years older	12. 4 years younger
5. 3 years older	13. 5 to 9 years younger
6. 2 years older	14. 10 to 15 years younger
7. 1 year older	15. 15 or more years younger
8. same age	

Mean scores of each occupational group support the hypothesis that administrators tend to be later born. The average ordinal birth position for administrators (superintendents and principals) was 2.9, while that for teachers was 2.4 and parents, 2.2.

COGNITIVE TRAITS

The effect of intelligence on administrative effectiveness has long been a point of speculation. Some observers feel that there is a range of optimal intelligence. An administrator must not be below a certain range or else the complexities of the job will prove overwhelming, but the higher ranges of intelligence may be more appropriate to theory and abstraction than to administration.

Similarity of intelligence is probably a factor in determining the citizen's response to an administrator. The results of the pilot study indicate considerable relation between intellectual compatibility and evaluation of administrative performance.

After trying several measures unsuccessfully, a test of intelligence appropriate for adults was finally found that combined the main features of general information, vocabulary, and logical reasoning. This test is a revision and shortening of the Terman Concept Mastery Test, which was published by the Psychological Corporation and used with their permission.

The measure of technical knowledge of educational administration was also used as a criterion measure and is presented in Chapter 4.

COGNITIVE STYLE

Recently there has been a great deal of interest in the way people perceive the world and attempt to come to terms with it. There are identifiable cognitive styles that may be looked upon as a supplement to interpersonal orientations. Another possible contributor to the rating of administrators is the similarity of cognitive styles of principal and interactor.

An adaptation of the Myers-Briggs Type Indicator (Myers, 1962) was selected as a measure of "cognitive style," or intellectual approach to the world. The instrument was constructed by Isabel Briggs Myers and Katharine C. Briggs. The Indicator is a self-report inventory that is intended to measure variables stemming from Jungian personality typology (Jung, 1923, 1953). It consists of four scales: Extraversion-Introversion (E-I), Sensation-Intuition (S-N), Thinking-Feeling (T-F), and Judging-Perceiving (J-P).

Two of these scales proved very successful in differentiating occupational groups in studies performed at the Institute of Personality Assessment and Research at the University of California (MacKinnon, 1962). They were extremely successful in measuring variables that appeared to contribute to success in one field of endeavor as opposed to another. The dimensions measured may thus be important predictors of success in a field like educational administration. These scales are defined as follows.

Judging-Perceiving. It is argued that a great part of overt cognitive activity can be regarded as either judging (coming to a conclusion about something) or perceiving (becoming aware of something); and that there are two ways of judging—thinking and feeling—and two ways of perceiving—sensation and intuition.

There is a fundamental difference between the attitudes. In the judging attitude, in order to come to a conclusion, perception must be shut off for the time being. The evidence is all in. Anything more is incompetent, irrelevant, and immaterial. One now arrives at a verdict and gets things settled. Conversely, in the perceptive attitude one shuts off judgment for the time being. The evidence is not all in. There is much more to it than this. New developments will occur. It is much too soon to do anything irrevocable (Myers, 1962).

Sensation-Intuition. The two modes of perception—sensation and intuition—can be described in the following way. There is not only the familiar process of *sensing*, by which we become aware of things directly through our five senses. There is also the process of *intuition*, which is indirect perception by way of the unconscious, accompanied by ideas or associations that the unconscious tacks on to the perceptions coming from outside. These unconscious contributions range from the merest masculine "hunch" or "woman's intuition" to the crowning examples of creative art or scientific discovery.

When people prefer sensing, they find too much of interest in the actuality around them to spend much energy listening for ideas out of nowhere. When people prefer intuition, they are too much interested in all the possibilities that occur to them to give much notice to the actualities (Myers, 1962).

These charming definitions, however, do not always correspond to the content of the items that comprise the instrument that measures them. Stricker and Ross (1963) found that "the Sensation-Intuition and Thinking-Feeling scales may reflect restricted aspects of the dimensions they are intended to represent, and the Extraversion-Introversion and Judging-Perceiving scales may reflect something quite different from their postulated dimensions."

For these reasons the tests were revised for this study.

Measurement: Imagination and Certainty

The original thirty to forty items on each scale were content analyzed for logical similarity. Several items were discarded and the remaining set renamed to be more consistent with the actual item content. The Intuitive-Perception scale was given the title *Imagination*, and the Feeling-Thinking scale was retitled *Certainty*.

The new items were put into a dichotomous answer form and administered to a group of 120 respondents. The items did not form a cumulative (Guttman) scale so they were subjected to an item analysis using the method of Ebel (1954) and also the traditional tetrachoric-r method. The best items were chosen from these methods and constituted the final scale.

CHAPTER 10

CORRELATION AND FACTORING OF MEASURES

INTERCORRELATION OF INDIVIDUAL MEASURES

A total of fifty-seven individual measures were used to predict the criteria of administrative effectiveness. These are referred to as *predictor variables*. As fifty-seven is a very cumbersome number to use for a study, and it is quite possible that there is some empirical intercorrelation among these variables even though they are theoretically independent, a factor analysis was done of these fifty-seven measures to reduce them to a more manageable number and to discover the interrelations among them.

Below are the original predictor variables used.

TYPE	NUMBER OF MEASURES
Cognitive Style (Imagination, Certainty)	2
Educational Values (VAL-ED)	14
Intelligence (Revised CMT)	1
Interpersonal Feelings (FIRO-F)	6
Defense Mechanisms (COPE)	5
Interpersonal Relations with Parents (LIPHE)	12
Biographical	10
Educational Background	3
Birth Order	4
TOTAL	57

Factor analyses were done for the total sample, and also for administrators and teachers separately. The results and the three analyses were compared and three factors selected. These factors were given names. The factor names and the predictor variables comprising the factor are given in Table 5.

TABLE 5.
Factors of Predictor Variables

Factor Name	Scale Title	Scale Name
1. I am dissatisfied with the way my father related to me.	*LIPHE IB (Fa)*	When I was a child, I wanted my father to spend more time with me and to give me more attention.
	LIPHE IB (Fa)	When I was a child, I wanted my father to be more interested in me and to feel more strongly that I was a significant person.
	LIPHE CF (Fa)	When I was a child, I wanted my father to have more respect for my ability to think and do things well.
2. I am dissatisfied with the way my mother related to me.	*LIPHE IB (Mo)*	When I was a child, I wanted my mother to spend more time with me and to give me more attention.
	LIPHE CG (Mo)	When I was a child, I wanted my mother to allow me more freedom and to allow me to think more for myself.
	LIPHE IF (Mo)	When I was a child, I wanted my mother to be more interested in me and to feel more strongly that I was a significant person.
	LIPHE CF (Mo)	When I was a child, I wanted my mother to have more respect for my ability to think and to do things well.
	LIPHE ABF (Mo)	When I was a child, I wanted my mother to show and to feel more love and affection for me.

TABLE 5 (Continued).

Factor Name	Scale Title	Scale Name
	LIPHE ICA (Mo)	When I was a child, my mother wanted me to be a better person.
3. I want people to notice, respect, and like me.	*FIRO-F w^I*	I want people to be interested in me, to pay attention to me, to feel I am important.
	FIRO-F w^C	I want people to respect and trust my competence and abilities.
	FIRO-F w^A	I want people to like me and to feel close and personal toward me.
4. I am interested in, respect, and like people.	*FIRO-F e^I*	I am interested in people and I think they are important and significant.
	FIRO-F e^C	I trust and respect other people's competence and abilities.
	FIRO-F e^A	I like people and I feel close and warm toward them.
5. I prefer conformity and conventionality.	*Certainty*	I prefer to do things in a scheduled, planned way rather than in a spontaneous unhampered fashion.
	Imagination (negative)	I prefer uniqueness and creativity as opposed to conventionality and practicality.
	VAL-ED TCm:C	The teacher should conform to the dominant values of the community.
	VAL-ED AT:C	The administrator should control the activities of the teacher, both in the classroom and in the community.
	VAL-ED ACm:C	The desires of the community should determine school policy.

TABLE 5 (Continued).

Factor Name	Scale Title	Scale Name
6. People in the school situation should have close and personal relations with each other.	*VAL-ED TCm:I*	The teacher should participate in community activities and be encouraged to do so by community members.
	VAL-ED TCm:A	The teachers and people in the community should be personally friendly with each other.
	VAL-ED AT:A	The administrator should be personally close with teachers and express feelings openly.
	VAL-ED ACm:I	The administrator and people in the community should be involved jointly in school and community affairs.
	VAL-ED ACm:A	The administrator and the people in the community should be personally friendly with each other.
7. Education is concerned with developing the whole child.	*VAL-ED importance*	Education has intrinsic value in and of itself beyond its utilitarian advantages.
	VAL-ED Mind (negative)	The school should concern itself primarily with the development of the minds of the students rather than with their whole personality.
	VAL-ED SC:C	The school should help students to realize and use their own abilities and judgement most effectively.
8. I am conservative.	*Politics*	My political views are conservative.

TABLE 5 (Continued).

Factor Name	Scale Title	Scale Name
	VAL-ED TC:A (negative)	The teacher should be personally friendly and warm toward the children.
	VAL-ED AT:I (negative)	The administrator should take account of teachers' opinions when making policy decisions.
9. I handle anxiety by attributing my unacceptable feelings and motives to others.	COPE Projection	I handle anxiety by attributing my unacceptable feelings and motives to others.
	COPE Turning against self (negative)	I handle anxiety by blaming myself unrealistically and punishingly.
10. I handle anxiety by denying the problem or its importance.	COPE Denial	I handle anxiety by denying the presence of a problem.
	COPE Isolation	I handle anxiety by acknowledging its presence but treating it intellectually.
	COPE Regression (negative)	I handle anxiety by turning to other people to solve my problem.
11. I am an established citizen.	Age	I am old.
	Income	I have a high income.
	Stability	I have lived in this community a long time.

FINAL FORM OF PREDICTOR VARIABLES

Factor analysis is very useful for reducing the fifty-seven scales to thirteen scores, but it does not preclude adding individual scale scores if there is a theoretical justification for their inclusion. Results of the factor analysis revealed that there were a few scales that did not fall clearly into any one factor but they seemed to be very useful or were of interest for particular reasons. For example, there is much interest in whether or not intelligence is related to administrative effectiveness; thus intelligence was included as a predictor variable.

Table 6 presents the complete list of the twenty-four predictor variables used in this study (eleven factors plus thirteen added individual items).

TABLE 6.
Final Form of Predictor Variables

No.	Name (content and positive end of scale)
1.	I am dissatisfied with the way my father related to me.
2.	I am dissatisfied with the way my mother related to me.
3.	I want people to notice, respect, and like me.
4.	I am interested in, respect, and like people.
5.	I prefer conformity and conventionality.
6.	People in the school situation should have close and personal relations with each other.
7.	Education is of importance in developing the whole child.
8.	I am conservative.
9.	I handle anxiety by attributing my unacceptable feelings and motives to others.
10.	I handle anxiety by denying the problem or its importance.
11.	I am an established citizen.
12.	I come from a large family.
13.	I have a high-status father.
14.	I am male.
15.	I am married.
16.	Religious preference.
17.	I am intelligent.
18.	I was a later born child in my family.
19.	The teacher should regulate classroom behavior.
20.	When I was a child, I wanted my father to allow me more freedom.
21.	My father wanted me to be a better person.
22.	I have held my position for many years.
23.	I have been a full-time teacher for many years.
24.	My teaching field tended toward the sciences and mathematics.

4

classification and sampling of school districts

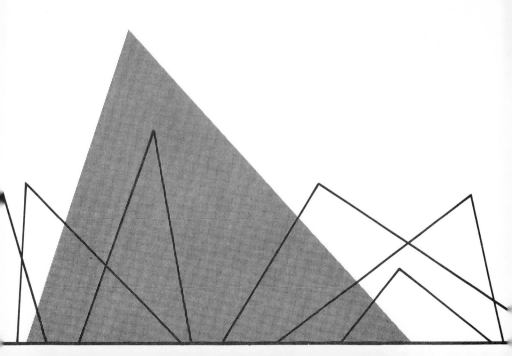

CHAPTER 11

CLASSIFICATION BY EXPERT JUDGES

In recent years, the behavioral sciences have moved steadily toward greater recognition of the importance of situational variables for the understanding and prediction of behavior. This recognition has led to an increasing number of research strategies that include both individual and situational factors.

In the chapters of Part 4,[1] a method is presented for selecting and classifying the sociological characteristics of the geographical units called school districts. School districts should be classified in such a way that a school administrator would perform with essentially the same effectiveness in any district within a particular category and differently from the way he would perform in any district in any other category.

A superintendent or principal may perform well in a large metropolitan area but fail in a small farm community. A school district composed of highly educated and vitally interested parents probably presents entirely different problems to an administrator than a district characterized by poorly educated and uninterested parents.

SELECTION OF VARIABLES

Two major approaches to identifying variables significant for administrator performance are the experiential and the objective. The experiential method uses the subjective experience of people familiar with the situation in educational administration and with the particular districts in question to classify the districts in terms of the aim of the classification. This method utilizes the pooled available knowledge of

---

[1]Part 4 was written with James R. Cameron, Rolf O. Kroger, and Frank Farner.

83

expert observers. The objective method involves deriving repeatable measures of the social characteristics of each school district—such as those measures listed in the census—and, through statistical methods, classifying districts into similar types.

If the empirical approach is used without the expert opinions, there can be little confidence that the resulting categories are related to, in this case, administrative effectiveness. They may be empirically discrete categories, easily reproduced, but have no validity whatever for discriminating administrative performance. On the other hand, expert judgment without empirical support remains subjective and limited. Other investigators may have difficulty repeating the procedure and the results would be quite unstable and probably unreliable.

In this study, both approaches were used and their results compared. If the results were different, those districts that came out differently would be examined to see if some dimensions were being omitted and corrections would be made. If the results of the classifications were sufficiently close, then the empirical method would be used, with confidence that it was both reliable and valid.

EXPLICATION

This method of utilizing expert opinions and then replacing them with an objective procedure has been described in the literature of the philosophy of science by Carnap (1950) as "explication"—a "transformation of an inexact, prescientific concept, the *explicandum*, into a new exact concept, the *explicatum*."

In this case the explicandum is the set of categories arrived at by expert opinion, a valuable piece of information but inexact and prescientific. The objectively derived set of district types is the explicatum.

The criteria Carnap gives for determining the adequacy of an explicatum are (1) similarity to the explicandum, (2) exactness, (3) fruitfulness, and (4) simplicity.

Comparing the results of classifications using the two methods is a means for maximizing the similarity of the explicandum and the explicatum. If there is little relation between the resulting typologies, clearly the objective method (explicatum) is not generating the same type of data that expert judges produce (explicandum). The criterion of fruitfulness can be met only through the use of the category system for empirical investigations, the main purpose of the present study. If the categories derived by the objective method actually produce district types in which similar kinds of administrators perform similarly and in which similar types of administrators perform differently in different district types, then the classification has demonstrated its fruitfulness for this type of study. The criteria of simplicity and exactness are met through the derivation of a simple, precise mathematical technique for classifying, unequivocally, any district into a district type. This chapter is devoted to deriving the explicandum from expert judges. In the following chapter an explicatum will be generated from empirical methods, and it will be demonstrated that the objective method (explicatum) is similar to the explicandum in that it is simple and exact and that there is face validity for its fruitfulness. The results of the study will provide empirical evidence for this fruitfulness.

SOME SAMPLING CONSIDERATIONS

For a study of administrative effectiveness to produce results relevant to the school situation in California, a sample must be selected of educational units representative of California, both on the average and with respect to the variability of educational settings. (In this study all references to the California school situation are to the early 1960's and the census data contained in the 1960 census.)

The usual method for selecting a representative subgroup from a large population is simple random sampling, that is, selecting a group of elements in such a way that each possible group has an equal chance of being selected for the sample. In most cases, a better method is to stratify the population and choose a random sample from within each stratum.

In order to stratify, both the individual units (districts, attendance areas) to be stratified and some of the important variables under investigation must be specified. Because a focus of the study is on interaction, it is important to have a sampling unit large enough to encompass all the people who have significant interaction with each other. For this purpose, the high school and the unified districts emerged as the most appropriate sampling unit. Stratification is aimed at dividing the high school and unified districts into strata that are homogeneous with respect to the various "conditions that lead to a given level of administrative effectiveness." Other districts and school attendance areas will be derived from these strata.

CLASSIFICATION PROCEDURES

Hansen, Hurwitz, and Madow (1953) stress the fact that the final determination of strata is a subjective matter and recommend that a large number of strata be developed.

With these guidelines in mind, it was decided to use the method of expert judges to stratify the high school and unified districts into as many strata as the experts found necessary.

A group of five experts[1] on the conditions in the public schools of California was assembled to classify the 339 union high school and unified school districts. The five were carefully selected so as to include at least two who knew each school district well. They met from 10 A.M. until 5 P.M. one day, working independently in the morning and as a group in the afternoon. After preliminary explanation and general discussion of the total project, each was given a deck of 339 cards, each card containing the name of a California unified or union high school district. These were to be classified into a moderate number of groups—somewhere between five and twelve. Each expert decided independently on a classification.

The basis of classification was administrative effectiveness. Each class represented districts where a given superintendent would operate with approximately equal effectiveness. If two districts appeared in different classes, this meant that a different set of personal characteristics were required for an administrator to operate at a given level of performance in one district than in another.

The term "administrative effectiveness" referred to the administrator's ability to create conditions under which children profit most from their school experience. Presumably this required effective community relations, teacher morale, and relations with the school board, as well as many other factors.

All judges finished their independent classifying by lunchtime. After a brief lunch they were asked to arrive at a mutually acceptable classification. Each person presented his classification and the basis for it, so that a variety of approaches were in evidence.

Results of the morning's independent classification revealed two major bases on which the judges had chosen to classify districts:

1. Demographic characteristics of the district, such as size, population density, chief industry, location, wealth.

2. Level of educational quality required by the district community from the superintendent. This level was felt to be a function of the educational sophistication of the community members, their concept of the type of school and program desired, and the degree of leadership expected from the superintendent.

During the course of the afternoon, the group decided to make two independent classifications using each of these criteria and later combine the two into one classification. The categories that were finally agreed upon are presented in Tables 7 and 8.

[1]Our thanks for the excellent work generously contributed by Hollis Allen, California State College at Fullerton; Robert Clemo and Floyd Taylor, California State Department of Education; Frank Farner, Claremont Graduate School; and Edgar Morphet, University of California, Berkeley.

TABLE 7.
Initial District Classification Systems
of Expert Judges: Demographic (DEM)

	Description	Number of Districts in Class
1.	Metropolitan city districts	5
2.	Large, cohesive city districts	12
3.	Large districts within a suburban sprawl	37
4.	Medium-size population centers with a dependent suburban or rural region	35
5.	Medium-size districts within a suburban sprawl	31
6.	Medium-size, cohesive town districts with no suburban or rural region	30
7.	Small districts (9th-12th grade ADA, 300-1000)	104
8.	Tiny districts (9th-12th grade ADA, under 300)	80
	Total	334 *

TABLE 8.
Initial Classification System of Expert Judges:
District Quality Requirement (DQR)

Two dimensions of three points each were used to generate a category classification.

Dimension I. Quality of Education Program Required of School (Program) High end is characterized by:

1. community demand for "culture" in schools and in superintendent;
2. community willingness to support schools adequately;
3. belief by community members that buildings are more than mere housing of pupils;
4. tradition of community and school board commitment to effectiveness in public schools.

	Description	Number of Districts in Class
High	District requires a high-quality school system	37
Medium	District requires an average-quality school system	157
Low	District makes no demands for quality and may even oppose attempts in that direction	140

*Kern County Union High School District was eliminated from the population as being unique, and four districts listed by the State Department of Education no longer existed: Raymond Granite, Sunnyside, Monrovia-Duarte, Citrus.

TABLE 8. (Continued).

Dimension II. Educational Leadership Required of Superintendent (Leadership) High end represents a district requiring a high degree of educational leadership, including breadth of interest and knowledge, experimentation, initiative, and innovation; and one that looks to the superintendent to keep the school system modern and in a leadership role.

	Description	Number of Districts in Class
High	District requires high degree of leadership from superintendent.	29
Medium	District requires average amount of leadership from superintendent	209
Low	District has no interest in educational leadership and may even oppose attempts at innovation by super-intendent.	99

What a district "required" was inferred in part from the types of superintendents it sought and hired and from the type of superintendent behavior it had or had not tolerated.

These two dimensions were combined, and each district was placed in one of the resulting nine classes.

TABLE 9.
Distribution of Districts in
District Quality Requirement (DQR) Classification

Program Description	Leadership Description	Designation	Number of Districts
High	High	1	13
High	Medium	2	24
High	Low	3	0
Medium	High	4	16
Medium	Medium	5	117
Medium	Low	6	24
Low	High	7	0
Low	Medium	8	65
Low	Low	9	75
		Total	334

Final Categories of Expert Judges

At this point, the committee of expert judges turned over to the present author the task of analyzing these classifications, finding their interrelations, and suggesting ways to the judges for combining the two schemes. The result of this process, the final categories of expert judges, is given in Table 10 below.

TABLE 10.
Final Categories of Expert Judges

Stratum	Description	Number of Districts
1.	Metropolitan city districts, high requirement for quality education (DQR).	5
2.	Big city districts, high DQR.	6
3.	Big city districts, medium DQR.	6
4.	Large suburban districts, high DQR.	11
5.	Large suburban districts, medium DQR.	22
6.	Large suburban districts, low DQR.	4
7.	Medium size population centers, high DQR.	8
8.	Medium size population centers, medium DQR.	25
8a.	(dropped) Medium size population center, low DQR.	(2)
9.	Medium size suburban district, high DQR.	9
10.	Medium size suburban district, medium DQR.	16
11.	Medium size suburban district, low DQR.	6
12.	Medium size cohesive towns (no suburbs), high DQR.	3
13.	Medium size cohesive towns (no suburbs), medium DQR.	22
14.	Medium size cohesive towns (no suburbs), low DQR.	5
15.	Small districts (300-1000 ADA), high DQR.	10
16.	Small districts, medium DQR.	64
17.	Small districts, low DQR.	30
17a.	(dropped) Tiny districts (300 ADA), high DQR.	(2)
18.	Tiny districts, medium DQR.	27
19.	Tiny districts, low DQR.	51
	Total	330

Strata 8a and 17a were dropped from the sample as being unique.

Selection of Sample

A prime requirement of a sample is that every unit has a known probability of being selected. This property allows for calculation of the
accuracy of estimates of the population made from the sample. In the
present stratified sample, a simple random sample was selected from
within each stratum. Size of the sample taken from any one stratum is,
in general, proportionate to the size of the stratum. However, one
problem arising from proportionate sampling is that samples from very
small strata are too small to be reliable. In order to avoid serious
underrepresentation it was decided, therefore, following Hansen,
Hurwitz, and Madow, to arbitrarily oversample the smallest sized
stratum. One further exception to sampling each stratum proportinate
to its size occurs for strata with a very large number of districts. In this
case, it is economical for the sample to be relatively smaller, since a
stable measure of that stratum can still be achieved without having to
take as many units as a proportionate sample would require.

These considerations led to different proportions of districts being
chosen from the various strata. Such a sample is called a *disproportionate stratified sample* and requires that, for any overall measure characterizing the total population, results obtained on sampled districts must
be weighed to retain the true population proportions.

To characterize the entire population on any one measure, the sum
of values on that measure for the sample districts within each stratum
must be multiplied by the stratum weight, these weighted values are
summed over all the strata and divided by the total number of districts
in the population.

Within each stratum the districts were ordered by decreasing high
school (ninth-to-twelfth grade) average daily attendance (ADA). The
sample was chosen by drawing random numbers for each stratum and
selecting the corresponding districts. For example, if a stratum had ten
districts, the districts within the stratum were arranged in order of
ADA, the district with the largest ADA being number one and the
smallest ADA number ten. If the random sample was to be of size three,
then three random numbers between one and ten were selected and
districts corresponding to these numbers were selected for the sample.
When a stratum was very large (strata 5, 8, 10, 13, 16, 17, 18, 19),
stratification on the basis of size was adopted to insure a good distribution of size within the stratum for those districts selected. This was
done by dividing the stratum into two substrata (or in the case of strata
16 and 19, three substrata) and selecting a subsample from within each
substratum. For example, in stratum 17 (30 districts) three random
numbers were chosen between 1 and 18 and two were chosen between
19 and 30, thus retaining the random procedure but inspiring a good
size distribution in the sample.

After the sample of districts was drawn, it was decided to distinguish the union from the unified high school districts. By this time, experience indicated that, for both the study of the superintendent and the study of the principal, it appeared to make a difference to performance whether the district was unified or union. Therefore, within each of the nineteen strata the union and unified districts should be sampled separately. However, an examination of the sample already chosen revealed that it was remarkably similar to the sample that would have been chosen if unified and union were sampled separately—so similar that little would be gained by resampling. The only change brought about by the introduction of the union-unified distinction, therefore, was to change the weights for each stratum.

From the design of the study it was clear that samples had to be chosen of several more administrative units in order to have a sample of the various types of administrators required. These units included high schools, junior high schools, and elementary schools. The same sampling principle used to select unified and union high school districts was used for these other units.

Adequacy of the Sample

Table 11 presents the sample and the population values for various size categories.

TABLE 11.
Population and Sample Size Characteristics

	Population	Sample
Number of High Schools and Unified Districts	334	73
Unified	122	36
Union High School	212	37
Number of Elementary School Districts	1,242	66
Number of High Schools	682	88
Number of Junior High Schools	326	42
Number of Elementary Schools	4,601	148
Total Number of Schools	5,609	278

A few comparative statistics were computed to determine how closely the sample approximates the population. These are presented in Table 12 (the p value represents the probability that a sample chosen from this population would have a greater difference from the population value than this sample, thus the higher the p value the better the sample).

TABLE 12.

Comparison of Sample and Population

	Population	Weighted Sample	p
Mean ADA	2,388	2,294	.93
Mean assessed valuation per ADA	44,807	49,624	.89
Mean expenditure per ADA	55,473	57,847	.97

Thus, the sample chosen seems to be a very good estimate of the population on these measures.

The purpose of stratification is to reduce the variance within the population by reducing the within-strata variability on a number of relevant variables. It is therefore appropriate to inquire about the degree to which the variance in fact was reduced by the stratification. The larger the reduction in variance, the greater the confidence that results obtained from the sample are applicable to the total population, and therefore the more likely a valid sample will be generated by using stratification.

The same three variables were selected to test the gain due to stratification: (1) size of district (as measured by 9 to 12 ADA), (2) wealth of district (as measured by assessed valuation per ADA), and (3) expenditures on schools (as measured by expenditure per ADA). These variables were chosen because they were felt to be relevant to administrator performance, were available for each school district, and the last two were relatively independent of the conscious basis used by the judges for stratification. The figures were provided by the Educational Research branch of the California Department of Education.

For size, stratification reduced the variance by 61 percent. Although this is quite a high reduction, it is not as impressive as it appears since the judges were consciously using ADA as one criterion for one (demographic) of their two bases for stratification.

For wealth of district, reduction in variance was 57 percent, a more impressive result since wealth was not one of the judges' criteria. The same may be said for expenditures, where stratification reduced the variance by 49 percent. Thus, by all three measures stratification resulted in a very substantial reduction in variance, thereby greatly increasing the reliability of inferences made from results obtained on the sample to characteristics of the total population of school districts in California.

These results mean that the same accuracy will be obtained with the stratified sample that would have been obtained with a random sample twice as large.

CHAPTER 12

CLASSIFICATION BY OBJECTIVE METHODS

Presumably the expert judges' basis for classification was related to the social structure of the community included within the school district. An objective characterization of the factors within the district community that pertain to education would seem to have face validity as an approximation of the bases for the judges' decisions, that is, a method of classifying school districts on a basis relevant to administrative effectiveness.

Review of the literature on the subject offers some guidelines for selecting community variables, although relatively little has been done in the study of social class factors in relation to education. Most studies delve deeply into the effects or contributions of education on particular social strata, without specifying how these classes are to be delimited.

Using these studies and our own personal experience with the school situation as a basis, the following analysis of the social situation was developed for use in the present project.

METHODS OF ASSESSING COMMUNITY VARIABLES

In addition to the expert ratings method that was discussed in the previous chapter, there are at least four methods of assessing community variables relevant to school administration. Some of these have been used in previous studies; others were developed for this project.

1. The power structure of the community.
2. The characteristics of the school board members.
3. The ability and willingness of the local district to pay for the school program (local support).
4. The community's sociological characteristics such as size, median age, income, education, and ethnic distribution.

Power Structure

Although a detailed description of power structure, especially one focused on types of pressures brought to bear on the school administrator, would be very valuable, it is not feasible for the present study. This investigation involves almost one hundred school districts and it would be extremely difficult to do a competent job of assessing the power situation for each. Such an analysis would be appropriate for a follow-up to the present project in which a few districts could be studied intensively to test the results obtained in the present study. It would also be useful for a longitudinal study of a small number of school districts.

School Board

School board membership is the most direct expression of community attitudes toward schools. Since most school boards are elected, it is reasonable to assume that board membership reflects the attitudes of the electorate. Further, since the school administrator works directly with the school board, board members represent an important aspect of the community situation for the administrator. Measurement of such properties as political attitudes, attitudes toward education, and longevity on the board would be very useful for describing the school situation.

It was intended that these measures be used for descriptive purposes; however, returns from school board members in the sample reached only about 50 percent. Since it is likely that there is a systematic difference between those who did return the questionnaires and those who did not, data available would not be a reliable method for characterizing school boards. While this method could not be used in the present study, the assessment of traits of board members is recommended for future studies when better returns from school boards are obtained.

Local Community Support

Since school districts exist largely as a result of local financing, one significant difference among district situations lies in the ability and willingness of the community to support a quality school program. In particular, the following relevant factors used in the study will be discussed and the methods for measuring them described.

Tax Wealth

A wealthy community has less difficulty being able to pay for a quality education program or for a good school administrator than does a poor community; therefore, the wealth of a community is very likely to influence administrator performance.

The Department of Education of the State of California in its annual fiscal report publishes the assessed valuation (AV) of each school district. For some districts the ratio of AV to the number of pupils in the school district is presented. The number of pupils is measured by the average daily attendance (ADA) for kindergarten through the twelfth grade (for unified districts). Hence, the figure used for available tax wealth is AV/ADA, which means roughly, the amount of wealth per student.

Since school-attendance figures are not published for individual areas, each attendance area within each school district was assigned the AV/ADA score attributed to its surrounding school district. This decision was justified by the fact that each school district is expected to share its actual and potential wealth equally among its constituent schools.

Each district is assessed at approximately 25 percent of the real value of its property. The percentage in California actually varies from 20 to 24 percent among the various counties (in 1962).

Valuations were weighted to take account of this discrepancy. All unified and all union high school districts in the state were ranked on AV/ADA and divided into deciles, and each district was given a number indicating the decile into which it fell. A decile score of zero meant that the district was in the lowest 10 percent of all California districts on AV/ADA. Decile nine indicated the highest 10 percent, and so on.

School Expenditure

The classification, current expenditures per ADA (CE/ADA), reports expenditures for essential educational services. It indicates the willingness of the community to use its wealth for school purposes. Measurement is complicated by the fact that elementary school pupils require less money than high school pupils for the same quality of education. The districts, then, were first divided into unified (kindergarten through twelfth grade) and union (nine through twelve, or seven through twelve), and deciles were derived for each type separately. Each district was assigned a decile score in the same manner as for AV/ADA.

SOCIOLOGICAL CHARACTERISTICS

A description of the school districts in terms of sociological characteristics was accomplished readily with the assistance of the 1960 Census of Population. The variables selected from the census for this study were age, race, marital status, income, education, occupation, school enrollment, and geographic mobility. Measures of each of these variables were obtained for each school district in the study.

Since the sampling units employed by the United States Census are not ordinarily identical with the sampling units used in the present study, it was necessary to find the census units that most closely approximated the various school districts. This was accomplished by placing a map of California school districts over the map of California census units and finding the census units best approximating each school district in the sample.

Each school district or school attendance area was converted into its equivalent census tract or standard metropolitan statistical area. Since school district boundaries rarely overlap with census tract boundaries, in order to match census areas with school districts, the following rules were adopted for the conversion.

1. If a district or attendance area covered three-fourths or more of a census tract, division, or standard metropolitan statistical area, the entire tract, division, or area was attributed to that school area.

2. If between one-fourth and three-fourths of a tract, division, or area was covered by a school, half of the total population of that census area was attributed to the school area.

3. If less than one-fourth of a census tract, division, or area fell within a particular school's or district's attendance area, that census area was disregarded.

4. If a single census unit covered two school attendance areas or districts, half of that census unit's population figures were attributed to both school areas.

Despite these rules, some errors of conversion remained unavoidable. For example, school district boundaries are often drawn to exclude certain elements of the population, such as minority groups, whereas the corresponding census tracts do not exclude such elements. There seemed to be no feasible way to eliminate this source of error.

This conversion was used to calculate values for the districts. For each school district, each measure was computed for the district's component census units and the average value derived. For example, to derive the median age of a school district, the median age of each census unit within the district was multiplied by the number of people in the census unit. These products were added across all component census units and divided by the total number of people in the district. The result was the median age of the school district.

Following is a description of each variable, why it was chosen, and the method used for measuring it.

Median Age

Information on age is obtained by the census through asking the question "When was this person born?" The data are presented in sixteen categories from which were calculated the average age for each school district.

Percent of Married People

Data on marital status are obtained by the census in four categories (single, married, widowed, and divorced) from which were calculated the percentage of the total married population of the school district.

School Enrollment Ratio

Data on school enrollment are tabulated separately for public and private (including parochial) schools and for the various levels of the public school systems: kindergarten, elementary, and high schools. From these data, an "enrollment ratio" was calculated, that is, the percentage of the total population of the district enrolled in the public schools. College enrollment data were excluded since this study is concerned with community interest in elementary and high school education.

School District Size

In addition to the school enrollment, the size of the school district makes a difference in the administration of the school. Size is usually measured by ADA. This information, supplied by the State Board of Education in its annual financial report, was used to classify districts by size.

Thus, for each district, there is a decile score, from zero to nine, computed for median age, for percent of married people, for enrollment ratio, and for size of school or school district (ADA).

Geographical Mobility

Stable patterns of residence are assumed to present fewer problems for the school administrator than fluctuating patterns, since the latter involve the difficult issues of integrating new members and separation from old friends. Communities characterized by fluctuating patterns of residence may show less involvement with the schools. Such communities should also require additional efforts on the part of the administrator to communicate ideas to the inhabitants of the district. In general, it is expected that different degrees of geographical mobility will present different problems for school administration.

Mobility was measured by dividing the number of people (over five years old) who left the county or standard metropolitan statistical area in the five-year period between 1955 and 1960 by the total number of people in the district in 1960. Again the scores are expressed as deciles with the higher number meaning greater mobility, or less stability.

Percent White

The implications of this variable for school administration in California center primarily around the usually lower socioeconomic status of minority group members and the possibility of racial tensions. School districts containing a large proportion of certain minority group members are usually faced with the consequences of a lack of motivation for school achievement, with the necessity of instituting remedial courses, with difficulties in the recruitment of teachers, and perhaps with more subtle problems attributable to relations between different racial groups. In the years subsequent to this study, this variable has become more timely and its measurement more crucial.

Information on race is obtained by the census through asking the respondent to classify himself in racial terms. The concept of race used by the census is "that which is commonly accepted by the general public." The census classifies the population into three racial groups: white, Negro, and other, including Orientals and American Indians. Persons of Mexican origin are classified in the first category. Since the interest here is in the relative number of members of the minority groups in each district, the percentage of white persons of the total population of the district will be used as the index of the racial composition of the district. These percentages are expressed as deciles with the higher numbers meaning a larger proportion of whites.

Personal Income and Variation in Income

Wealthy people notably have different attitudes about school finances than do poor people. It is difficult to predict the direction of this difference, but it seems a sufficiently potent factor to merit careful investigation.

The census obtains information about income through asking the respondent to report his "total income." From the resulting distribution, the median income of the district was obtained as well as the semi-interquartile range as a measure of the variability in incomes in the different districts. Variability seems important since it reflects the degree to which the district contains both rich and poor (high variability) as opposed to having persons of approximately equal incomes (low variability).

The median income and the variability of income within the district were both converted to deciles with a high score meaning high income and high variability, respectively.

Education

Attitudes toward education are often related to one's own education. Diverging attitudes in this area could be very influential in determining the kind of administrator who will succeed in a given district.

Information about education was obtained through census questions asking for the highest grade (or year) of school attended and if this grade (or year) was finished.

The census data included the median number of years of school completed for persons twenty-five years old and over. This figure was converted to deciles with the higher score designating a district with a larger median number of years of schooling completed, that is, a more highly educated district.

Occupation and Variation in Occupation Level

The occupational pattern of a community often determines its values and attitudes toward education, and is also related to its expectations of the person who is to be a school administrator. For example, a community of college professors may want a different kind of person and a different performance from a school administrator than a community of lumbermen or of farmers.

The classification of occupations is much more complex than the classification of the previously discussed variables. Income, for example, is easy to classify because it is quantitative along one scale. But occupations, by and large, are simply diverse, and differ from each other along many dimensions and, therefore, pose a difficult problem for arraying them along one continuum.

The classification developed for the present study is based upon the skill requirements of the occupation and the prestige value of the occupation.

Occupations were selected from the census list and arranged in descending order into seven levels. The occupations were placed in that order first on the basis of skill required and then, independently, on the basis of their prestige value, as ascertained by the North-Hatt

Scale (1961). These two independent classifications resulted in highly similar groupings. The seven levels are:

Level 7. Higher Professional. Occupations requiring a high degree of intellectual ability and activity. The work is typically concerned with theoretical and practical aspects of complex fields of human endeavor and requires prolonged training and experience. In prestige, these occupations are equivalent to the top thirty occupations on the North-Hatt Scale. For managerial personnel, the number of persons supervised constitutes the criterion for placing a given person at one of the levels. Examples: physician, university professor (but not junior college professor), colonel, author ("serious," free-lance).

Level 6. Middle Professional. As above, but less demanding with respect to background or the need for initiative and judgment in complex work situations. Area of competence is typically more restricted than Level 7 occupations. Examples: pharmacist, ship captain, advertising agent, elementary school principal.

Level 5. Lower Professional. As above, but even more restricted with respect to background or the need for initiative and judgment and area of competence. Examples: reporter, surveyor, librarian, nurse.

Level 4. Supervisors and Technicians. Occupations involving supervision of others at the "first-line" level and usually requiring possession of technical knowledge on the part of the supervisor, as well as occupations requiring the highest degree of some technical skill. Examples: construction foreman, factory foreman, lithographer, private secretary, cabinetmaker.

Level 3. Skilled Workers. Occupations requiring predominantly a comprehensive knowledge of work processes, exercise of judgment, and responsibility for valuable products and/or equipment. Examples: machinist, automobile repairman, stenographer, bookkeeper.

Level 2. Semi-skilled Workers. Occupations requiring a high degree of manual dexterity and alertness in a well-defined work context where unusual problems are referred to others. Examples: bus driver, practical nurse, lumberman, corporal. These occupations are roughly equivalent to those found on the North-Hatt Scale at ranks 62-75.

Level 1. Unskilled Workers. Occupations requiring usually heavy manual labor and little previous experience in the specific occupation. These occupations are equivalent to the fifteen occupations ranked at the bottom of the North-Hatt Scale. Examples: farm laborer, longshoreman, porter, janitor.

Using this classification, levels were assigned to each of the following U.S. Census occupation categories.

Professional, technical, and kindred workers (7)
Managers, officers, and proprietors, including farm (6)
Clerical and kindred workers (3)
Sales workers (3)
Craftsmen, foremen, and kindred workers (4)
Operatives and kindred workers (2)
Private household workers (2)
Service workers except private household (2)
Laborers, except mine (1)
Occupation not reported

Each school district was characterized by mean occupational level, obtained by weighting the level of each occupational group by the number in that group, and the variation in occupational level in the district measured by the semi-interquartile range of the resulting distribution. The latter measure gives an estimate of the homogeneity of occupation levels in the community. The scores were converted to deciles with the high scores meaning, respectively, high status occupations and high diversity of occupation within the district.

DISTRICT TYPE PROFILES

The first step in assigning a school district to a district type is to compute its decile scores on each dimension. This profile of scores of the district is then compared to the profile of each district type. The district is assigned to the type it fits best.

For practical purposes, it is not necessary to compute the mean decile scores separately for each type and then find the average. The same result is achieved by comparing the decile scores of a district on each variable with the scores of each district cluster and choosing the one best fit, providing modifications of this simple procedure are made: a) some variables are not counted since they do not fall into any type (e.g., mobility, occupation level, for the unified district analysis), b) some variables are counted more than once since they arrear in more than one variable dimension (e.g., median age—appears on dimensions 2 and 4—in unified district analysis). Table 13 presents the profiles of each district type.

The mean distance for each district from the ideal type profiles is then computed and the district placed in the type it mostly closely approximates. Table 14 shows this computation for the best definers of each cluster.

TABLE 13.

Unified Districts: Object Analysis
Profile of District Types

District Types	Enrl	Educ	Mob	Inc	VInc	Occ	VOcc	Age	Mar	Wht	Size	Wlth	Xpnd
1	1	6	•	5	6	•	3	7	1	1	8	7	7
2	5	7	•	9	5	•	2	5	7	7	5	4	5
3	4	4	•	5	3	•	4	3	3	2	7	2	4
4	4	2	•	1	6	•	5	8	5	6	0	8	8
5	7	1	•	2	2	•	9	3	5	5	3	3	0

Entries are decile scores, • means variable is not used for classification in this analysis.

TABLE 14.

Unified and Union High School Districts:
District Type Profiles for Best
Definers of Each District Type

District Type 1

District	Distances from profiles of cluster.				
	1	2	3	4	5
Acalanes	0.8	2.9	4.2	0	5.5
Temple City	0.9	2.8	3.4	3.3	3.3
Culver City	0.9	2.6	2.9	2.5	3.2
South Bay	0.9	2.5	4.0	0	5.0
Covina Valley	1.2	2.8	4.9	4.6	3.3
Mean	0.9	2.7	3.8	3.5	4.1

District	Distances from profiles of cluster.				
	1	2	3	4	5
Vallejo	2.4	1.0	4.2	3.1	2.4
Stockton	3.4	1.5	3.9	2.6	2.7
San Diego	2.7	1.2	4.2	2.0	3.4
Grant	3.6	2.1	4.3	0	3.5
Lincoln	2.8	1.5	2.3	0	3.4
Mean	3.0	1.5	3.8	2.6	3.1

TABLE 14. (Continued).

District Type 3

	Distances from profiles of cluster.				
District	1	2	3	4	5
King City	3.8	2.5	0.6	0	3.1
Oro Madre	2.9	3.8	0.9	3.2	3.0
Middletown	3.8	4.5	1.0	3.7	3.7
Calistoga	3.5	3.5	1.2	3.5	3.6
Gustine	3.5	3.2	1.3	0	3.4
Mean	3.5	3.5	1.0	3.5	3.3

District Type 4

	Distances from profiles of cluster.				
District	1	2	3	4	5
Oakland	3.0	2.3	3.0	0.8	4.3
San Francisco	3.5	2.6	3.3	1.0	4.8
Pasadena	3.1	3.2	3.7	1.1	5.5
Santa Monica	3.2	2.9	3.0	1.2	4.9
Los Angeles	3.2	2.3	3.5	1.2	4.3
Mean	3.2	2.6	3.3	1.1	4.7

District Type 5

	Distances from profiles of cluster.				
District	1	2	3	4	5
Delano	5.6	3.8	3.1	0	0.8
Fowler	5.3	3.5	2.7	0	0.8
Folsom	3.5	2.7	3.4	4.8	0.8
Corona	2.8	2.7	3.3	4.6	0.9
Clovis	3.5	2.5	4.0	4.8	0.9
Mean	4.1	3.0	3.3	4.7	0.8

The precision with which the type is defined may be estimated with two measures. The mean distance score of all districts from the district type to which they belong indicates how closely they fit the district type—a lower score means a closer fit.

The uniqueness with which the defining districts fit their district type is measured by the difference between how well they fit their district type and how well they fit the second closest district type. Table 15 presents these data.

TABLE 15.

Measures of Precision of District Types

District	Mean best fit	Mean difference from second best fit
1	0.94	1.76
2	1.46	1.26
3	1.00	2.16
4	1.06	1.78
5	0.84	1.90

These figures indicate that all district types are about equally well defined except cluster two which is considerably less clear. The districts in Type 2 do not fit as well into the type, and they fit closer to some other type.

VARIABLES DESCRIBING DISTRICTS

The variables used to describe school districts and school attendance areas by the objective method are given below.

1. School enrollment ratio
2. Education
3. Geographical mobility
4. Personal income
5. Income variation
6. Occupation level
7. Occupation variation
8. Median age
9. Percent married
10. Percent white
11. School (district) size
12. Tax wealth
13. School expenditures

CHAPTER 13

COMPARISON: EXPERT JUDGES' RATINGS AND OBJECTIVE METHODS

It is now possible to compare the results of the objective analysis with the ratings by the expert judges.

Table 16 gives the strata assigned by judges to the five best definers of each type and the mean strata rating for each district type.

TABLE 16.

Unified and Union High School Districts:
Experts' Ratings of Five Best Definers of
Objective District Types

Objective District Type	District	Judges' Stratum
1	Acalanes	4
	Temple City	11
	Culver City	11
	South Bay	6
	Covina Valley	9
	Mean =	8.2
2	Vallejo	3
	Stockton	2
	San Diego	1
	Grant	5
	Lincoln	7
	Mean =	3.6

TABLE 16 (Continued).

Objective District Type	District	Judges' Stratum
3	King City	16
	Oro Madre	18
	Middletown	19
	Calistoga	19
	Gustine	18
	Mean =	18.0
4	Oakland	1
	San Francisco	1
	Pasadena	2
	Santa Monica	2
	Los Angeles	1
	Mean =	1.4
5	Delano	13
	Fowler	16
	Folsom	13
	Corona	14
	Clovis	13
	Mean =	13.8

District Type 4 represents mainly the metropolitan or large suburban districts, while Type 1 consists primarily of suburban districts. Type 3 comprises very small communities, and Type 2 is made up mainly of population centers somewhat removed from metropolitan areas (except San Diego). Type 5 comprises moderate-size districts harder to characterize.

The five district types represent very different points on the expert judges' ratings. The average strata scores of defining districts for each type make a progression along the judges' strata (It should be kept in mind that the judges' strata only approximate a continuum, but viewing them as such is a sufficient approximation for comparison to the objective district types.): 1.4, 3.6, 8.2, 13.8, 18.0. Types 3, 4, and 5 are very homogeneous with respect to strata, and types 1 and 2 are almost as good. The district types seem to have selected out various subgroups of strata along the range of the strata defined by the judges. There can be little doubt that the objective district types represent educationally significant divisions.

FINAL CLASSIFICATION

The close similarity of the cluster analysis method applied to the objective data and the expert judges' ratings justifies the use of the objective method as the basis for classifying districts. Checking personally with some of the judges about the objective classification reinforced the impression of this similarity. Therefore, for the reasons discussed earlier, the objective analysis was used in this study for district and school classification.

One further refinement was made before the method of classification was complete. Classifying a district by placing it in the district type it fits best is a rather gross procedure, since some districts fit much better than others. Good examples, in the unified district analysis, are the districts of Culver City, San Diego, Sierra, and Coronado. Computation following the classification procedure revealed that Culver City fit District Type 1 very well and fit no other type well. San Diego fit Type 2 quite well, but fit District Type 4 almost as well. Sierra did not fit any type very well, but it clearly fit better into Type 3 than in the others. And Coronado did not fit any type well but fit two clusters almost equally well. Thus, a combination of how closely a district fit its closest district type and how well it fit that type compared to how well it fit the other types provided a second method of classifying the districts.

Examination of the distribution of scores led to the following definitions of good fit for unified districts: "fits closest type well," "not close," "unique fit," and "not unique," and these characteristics were included in the classification scheme.

At this point our study yielded descriptions of final district types.

DESCRIPTION OF FINAL DISTRICT TYPES

Type 1, Suburban: located primarily around Los Angeles and around San Francisco (Culver City, Covina Valley, Acalanes).

Six of the first seven districts of this classification are in Los Angeles County. Probably the reason more suburban districts around San Francisco are not included is the vicissitudes of sampling. The surrounding counties of Contra Costa, San Mateo, and Alameda were represented by only three districts (plus Oakland) while Marin County was not represented in the sample. District Type 1 was very clear cut.

Type 2, Population centers: somewhat removed from metropolitan areas (Vallejo, Stockton, Lincoln).

These districts tend to be centers of population outside of the suburban sprawl. Sometimes they are the largest town in a farm community, for example. Districts of various sizes fell into this type, from very small to as large as San Jose and San Diego. This type was not as sharply defined as most of the others.

Type 3, Very small communities: (Middleton, Calistoga, Gustine).

This category is very well defined. These districts are the smallest in the state, most having an ADA of around 300.

Type 4, Metropolitan and large suburban areas: (San Francisco, Los Angeles, Pasadena).

A very well-defined type.

Type 5, Moderate size districts: not near a metropolitan area (Delano, Folsom, Clovis).

Most of these districts are in medium-sized cohesive towns with no suburbs, away from metropolitan centers. They fit between the small towns (Type 3) and the population centers (Type 2). This type is very homogeneous on the judges' ratings.

DISTRICT PARTICIPATION

Seventy-two unified and union high schools were invited to participate and 71 percent responded with at least the superintendent or a board member filling out the questionnaire. Accepting an invitation to participate represented a tremendous investment in time and energy by a district, because it entailed filling out a two-hour questionnaire by all board members, superintendent, staff, some principals, all teachers, and parents. Thus, 71 percent represents a remarkable achievement and speaks in a bold voice for the spirit of cooperation of the large majority of school districts in California, and of the members of the universities and educational organizations represented on the California Commission on Public School Administration.

From the standpoint of sampling, the results are reasonably satisfactory. The rule of thumb used by many sampling statisticians (Madow, personal communication) is that an 85 percent sample is ideal, a 60 percent sample is unsatisfactory, and between these limits it is difficult to judge.

Within the school districts accepting, the percentage of every category of respondent was very high (above 90 percent) except for school board members (about 50 percent) and of course parents, who were not actually sampled.

The sample selected originally was deliberately overchosen, that is, more were chosen than were needed for the sample, specifically because it was feared that there would be many refusals. Whether this overchoice improves the sample over the smaller number that could have been selected depends upon whether or not there were systematic biases in the type of districts that accepted.

Analysis reveals a similar distribution of acceptances throughout all strata and all district types except for the metropolitan districts

(District Type 4). Clearly the sample was weak in the large metropolitan areas. This is partly due to the fact that there are far fewer metropolises than small districts and one or two refusals at this level drastically decreases the percent accepting. Anticipating this possibility, all five large-city districts in stratum 1 were invited to participate instead of only a sample, and two of the five accepted. Thus the number of large districts in the sample is proportionate to the number of districts in the sample from the other strata, but the representativeness is suspect. It is possible statistically, and probably impressionistically, that districts refusing to participate are qualitatively different in the type of administrative situation presented to the administrator from those that accepted the invitation to participate.

The pattern of acceptance for the remaining districts is roughly the same with a slight rise in the percent accepting as the districts approach the higher numbered strata—the smaller districts.

In summary, the sample, for this type of study, is very satisfactory and there can be considerable confidence that results of this study are applicable to all of California. The only exceptions to this statement are the very large metropolitan districts that are too few to be well sampled and that are not adequately represented in this sample. Perhaps they must be studied separately since they are very complex and unique, and many of these districts actually contain several district equivalents within them.

SUMMARY

Selecting a representative sample of California school districts and classifying districts into types that related to administrative performance present very similar problems. Both require a grouping of school districts into types distinguished by the different situations they presented to school administrators and, therefore, indicate different administrative performances expected within each type of district.

Two methods of classification were used and integrated: (1) the experiential method drawing on the expert judges' knowledge of California schools, and (2) the objective method using a statistical treatment (key cluster analysis) of a variety of carefully selected objective measures of community characteristics taken from the 1960 United States Census and the annual financial report of the California State Department of Education.

Sampling the school districts of California was accomplished by selecting a disproportionate random sample from each of nineteen strata of unified and high school districts, developed by the expert judges. A similar method was used to select elementary school districts and attendance areas for elementary, junior high, and high schools. The sample chosen approximated very closely the total population of school districts in California on three measures used to test the quality of fit of the sample: (1) school district size, (2) tax wealth, and (3) school expenditures. The stratification reduced the variation on these measures by about 50 percent, meaning that the results achieved with this sample are equivalent to those that would be obtained with a random sample twice as large.

The objective method of classifying districts using cluster analysis produced district types very similar to those produced by the expert judges. This objective method was therefore used to classify districts into types that were homogeneous with respect to the social situations afforded school administrators. The three major variables used for this classification were land, wealth, and social status of community members. From these variables three to five types were generated, depending on the category of district or level of school, and every district and school was assigned to one type. A method was presented for classifying any school district into a district type.

Of all the unified and union high school districts invited to participate in the study, 71 percent accepted the invitation (fifty-one out of seventy-two). Of those that accepted, virtually all of the administrators and teachers and about half of the school board members actually filled out the two-hour questionnaire. Analysis of the pattern of acceptance revealed that the sample satisfactorily represented all of California's school districts except for the large metropolitan area districts. Only two out of the five districts in stratum 1 participated so that the application of the present results to this type of district is not justified.

If the results of this study are to be applied to another school area or if the research is replicated at a different time, the district classification would have to be redone to be current. It is possible, however, that many of the variables used for classification transcend time and space. In itself, that possibility is intriguing, but, of course, it requires empirical exploration through cross-validation.

5

conclusions
and recommendations

CHAPTER 14

RESULTS

A major purpose of this study is to interrelate three sets of variables—individual traits, social settings, and administrator effectiveness ratings—in order to acquire data to fit the basic formula of the investigation: *Administrator A is rated R on effectiveness criterion C in situation S.* Following is a summary of the measures of the major variables.

CRITERIA OF ADMINISTRATIVE EFFECTIVENESS

For Principal

Overall rating (Rtg): the assessment of a principal's effectiveness as compared to other principals known to the raters (average of all ratings given by principal's teachers).

Personal traits (Pers): the qualities characteristic of a principal's personal performance, including problem-solving ability, ability to maintain school plant, and educational leadership.

Organizational traits (Org): the ability to integrate and coordinate various elements of school situation into efficient operation, including organizational efficiency, ability to use human resources well, and skill in communication.

Interpersonal traits (IP): satisfaction with interpersonal situation that a principal elicits from teachers, staff, and board members; the degree to which raters feel that the principal finds them important, competent, and likeable.

Task ability (Task): combination of personal and organizational traits; the sum of all task-ability scales used to assess administrative performance.

Technical knowledge (TK): knowledge of topics such as school law, school finance, and school building.

For Superintendent

Overall rating (Rtg): general administrative effectiveness.

Problem solving (Prb): the degree to which efficient solution of our school district problems is facilitated.

Communication (Com): the degree to which an effective system of communication is maintained through school district.

Educational leadership (Ldr): the degree to which a superintendent provides a high level of educational leadership.

School maintenance (Mnt): the degree to which such matters as schedules, building maintenance, and availability of teaching materials are dealt with efficiently.

Organization (Org): the degree to which activities are organized to obtain maximum benefit from district resources.

Use of human resources (Res): the degree to which school personnel feel motivated, prepared, and given an opportunity to do their best for school district.

Board relations (Brd): the degree to which a superintendent deals effectively with the school board.

Technical knowledge (TK).

INDIVIDUAL TRAITS

Following are the characteristics (Predictor Variables) measured for each administrator and used for prediction.

Name (content and positive end of scale)

1. I am dissatisfied with the way my father related to me.
2. I am dissatisfied with the way my mother related to me.
3. I want people to notice, respect, and like me.
4. I am interested in, respect, and like people.
5. I prefer conformity and conventionality.
6. People in the school situation should have close and personal relations with each other.
7. Education is concerned with developing the whole child.
8. I am conservative.
9. I handle anxiety by attributing my unacceptable feelings and motives to others.
10. I handle anxiety by denying the problem or its importance.
11. I am an established citizen.

12. I come from a large family.
13. I have a high-status father.
14. I am male.
15. I am married.
16. I prefer a high-status religion.
17. I am intelligent.
18. I was a later born child in my family.
19. The teacher should regulate classroom behavior.
20. When I was a child, I wanted my father to allow me more freedom.
21. My father wanted me to be a better person.
22. I have held my position for many years.
23. I have been a full-time teacher for many years.
24. My teaching field tended toward the sciences and mathematics.

SITUATIONAL VARIABLES

District Types

Type 1. *Small, suburban:* located around large metropolitan areas such as Los Angeles and San Francisco (Culver City, Acalanes).

Type 2. *Population centers:* somewhat removed from metropolitan areas (Stockton, Vallejo).

Type 3. *Very small:* districts within very small communities (Calistoga, Middletown).

Type 4. *Metropolitan and large suburban:* (San Francisco, Pasadena).

Type 5. *Moderate:* medium size districts, not near metropolitan areas (Delano, Folsom).

The final number of administrators with usable data by district types is given in Table 17.

Because of sample size, union and unified, and high school, junior high, and elementary school administrators were combined by district type. The four types of studies were, therefore, not separately analyzed. Having the design in that form maximized proportional representation from each group.

The number of superintendents in each district was too small to do a regression analysis except for District Type 2. Therefore, for analytic purposes, all superintendents were treated as one group and regression analysis was done on the total.

The size of the principal groups was sufficient for regressions on District Types 1, 2, and 3, allowing for a test of the hypothesis that prediction of administrative success is improved by controlling for district type. This hypothesis may be checked further by the use of the one district type with a sufficient number of superintendents—District Type 2.

TABLE 17.
Final Population of Administrators

District Type	Superintendents	Principals
1	17	35
2	29	61
3	20	36
4	3	4
5	8	11
Total administrators = 224	77	147

INDIVIDUAL PREDICTORS OF CRITERIA

The first stage of prediction answers the question "How well are the criteria of effectiveness predicted by the individual predictor variables?" The effectiveness criteria were derived in three ways:

1. Ratings for principals derived from teachers' evaluations;
2. Ratings for some superintendents derived from school board members' evaluations;
3. Ratings for some superintendents derived from evaluations made by staff members.

Each of these methods of obtaining ratings was analyzed separately for each of the effectiveness criteria. The most direct measure of the predictability of these criteria is the partial correlation of each predictor variable with each criterion, that is, the correlation of each variable holding all other predictor variables constant. All correlations were made positive by reversing scale names when correlations were negative.

The results indicate the relative inability of the individual predictor variables to predict the various criteria of administrative effectiveness for principals. Only 9 correlations out of a possible 144 (6 percent) were above .20, and of those 9 one predictor accounted for 4 of the correlations.

That particular variable, *years of full-time teaching*, is of interest because it is *negatively* related to administrative success. This finding, supported strongly by subsequent analyses, is directly contrary to the legal requirement in many states that is based on the assumption that administrators require considerable teaching experience. In California, for example, five years of full-time teaching is a prerequisite for an administrative credential. These results indicate that this requirement is not only unjustified but may act *against* selecting good administrators.

Making an analysis of predictability for superintendents required the combining of all superintendents, whether rated by board members, or by staff members, or by both, because of the relatively small numbers involved.

Again individual prediction was poor, only twenty-three out of 216 correlations (11 percent) exceeded .20. The best predictors of administrator success as rated by board members and/or staff members were:

The administrator is not conservative.

The administrator wants people to notice, respect, and think well of him.

The administrator is an early born child in a large family.

The first two factors may be interpreted as a liberal attitude toward people and a sensitivity to their reactions. The last named trait seems reasonable in that large families require administration and organization in order to get their work done, and the older children—that is, the earlier born—are generally given major responsibility for organizing the other children to accomplish the necessary work. Thus these children have had much "administrative" experience by the time they reach adulthood.

Dividing superintendents into those rated by school board members and those rated by staff reveals many interesting differences.

The results of the ratings by board members are somewhat higher than the prediction of principal effectiveness. Three correlations go as high as .42 and, of the 288 possible correlations, fifty-four (19 percent) are above .20. Of the fifty-four correlations, no one predictor stands out as clearly better overall. The most frequent predictor variables are:

The administrator wants people to notice, respect, and think well of him.

The administrator comes from a large family.

The correlations that resulted from staff ratings were still higher than they were for the previous two ratings, reaching a high of .73. Furthermore, 92 out of 216 (43 percent) of the correlations were above .20. The most highly chosen predictors were:

The administrator is not conservative.

The administrator wants to be noticed, respected, and liked by people.

The administrator is not conformist or conventional.

The administrator thinks teachers should regulate classroom behavior.

Two particularly interesting results emerge from these analyses: (1) predictability of administrative performances from predictor variables increases as ratings go from teachers, to board members, to staff; and (2) different predictors "work" for each rating group.

Apparently, predictability increases as the homogeneity of the rating group's concept of an ideal administrator increases and as the working proximity of the rating group with the administrator increases. From this hypothesis, it follows that staff members are more in agreement on what they want from a superintendent, and because they work closer to him, they can tell better whether or not he has the traits they want. It also follows that board members are in less agreement about their criteria for a good superintendent, and having less direct contact with him, they have less opportunity to see if he has the desired traits. Teachers are most heterogeneous with regard to requirements for a principal and perhaps have less opportunity for close contact with him, especially in large schools.

The fact that different predictors are better for predicting what teachers, staff, and board members want from an administrator gives some insight into these relations. The administrator rated high by teachers, rather surprisingly, tends to be someone who did not teach a very long time and does not believe in close, personal relations in the school setting. The administrator rated high by board members, wants people to think well of him and tends to be a later born child in a large family. Staff members rate high an administrator who is liberal, somewhat nonconformist, feels teachers should regulate classroom activities, and wants people to think highly of him.

MULTIPLE PREDICTORS OF ADMINISTRATIVE SUCCESS

The second method of predicting administrative success is to weight all predictor variables in such a way that the weighted total of all variables yields the maximum correlation with the criterion—the multiple regression method. The method usually increases the correlation over any single variable.

The results of the regression analysis are given in Table 18.

TABLE 18.

Multiple Correlations of Predictor Variables with Criterion Variables for Superintendents Rated by Board Members (N=71), Superintendents Rated by Staff (N=46), and Principals Rated by Teachers (N=147)

Criteria

	TK	Rtg	Res	Prb	Com	Ldr	Brd	Mnt	Org	Mean
Superintendent	74	60	63	58	59	59	61	49	48	59
by Board	(42)	(31)	(42)	(26)	(30)	(29)	(32)	(22)	(25)	(31)
Superintendent	77	84	80	77	78	84	92	79	77	81
by Staff	(41)	(51)	(49)	(46)	(58)	(56)	(73)	(56)	(46)	(53)

	TK	Rtg	Pers	Org	IP	Task	Mean
Principal	50	47	45	42	45	43	45
by Teachers	(33)	(22)	(20)	(20)	(23)	(20)	(23)

Numbers in parenthesis are the highest partial correlations of the criterion with any individual predictors. Comparison of the individual correlations reveals that there is a sizable correlation, or predictive power, of the multiple correlation over the best individual predictor. These increments vary in the board-rated superintendents from .21 to .32, with a mean of .28; in the staff-rated superintendents from .19 to .36, with a mean of .28; and in the principals from .17 to .25, with a mean of .22. Thus, on the average, the multiple correlation improves the predictive power about .26 correlation points, a considerable increment.

There is one reservation in the use of multiple correlation however. With the large number of predictor variables used, it becomes easier to weight them in a manner that obtains a correlation higher than would be obtained on a fresh sample. For that reason the multiple correlation may be adjusted to take account of that property. The adjusted correlation represents an estimate of the lower bound of what the correlation would be on a new sample. Adjusted correlations are given in Table 19.

Multiple correlations in new populations may, of course, be even higher than those found on this sample. The adjusted correlations provide a statistical caution for generalizing these results.

MULTIPLE CORRELATIONS CONSIDERING TYPES OF SCHOOL DISTRICTS

If a given predictor variable is positively related to good administration in one district type, but negatively related to good administration in a different type of district, the prediction of administrative effectiveness for all districts will be low, thus masking the real situation. Multiple correlations computed within district types should be higher since the variable will act the same in every district within each type.

Multiple correlations were, therefore, computed within district types. As mentioned above, the size of the sample allowed this to be done only for principals in District Types 1, 2, and 3, and for superintendents in District Type 2. The multiple correlations within district types are presented in Table 20.

TABLE 19.
Adjusted Multiple Correlations (Lower Bound)
Criteria

	TK	Rtg	Res	Prb	Com	Ldr	Brd	Mnt	Org	Mean
Superintendent by Board	28	31	44	40	42	40	42	39	31	37
Superintendent by Staff	36	60	49	36	41	60	83	46	36	50

	TK	Rtg	Pers	Org	IP	Task	Mean
Principal by Teachers	21	24	17	17	24	17	20

TABLE 20.
Multiple Correlations of Predictor Variables with Criterion Variables for Principals, by District Type
Criteria

		TK	Rtg	Pers	Org	IP	Task	Mean
District Type	1	71	87	95	91	95	93	88
District Type	2	63	57	62	68	48	65	60
District Type	3	94	87	85	91	93	89	90

Again, because of sample size there is a possibility of spuriously high multiple correlations. Adjusted correlations take account of the small sample size and represent the lower limit of the correlation if done on a larger sample. Adjusted correlations are presented in Table 21.

TABLE 21.

Adjusted Multiple Correlations (Lower Bound) for Principals by District Type

				Criteria				
		TK	Rtg	Pers	Org	IP	Task	Mean
District Type	1	42	60	57	52	60	54	54
District Type	2	01	00	00	32	00	40	12
District Type	3	42	49	67	62	49	65	56

Even with the adjusted scores, District Types 1 and 3 are very strong while District Type 2 is unstable. This result probably reflects the fact that District Type 2 was not as well defined as the others.

Figure 1 presents a graphic representation of the improvement in prediction due to the introduction of district types.

Improvement in predictability is consistent for all districts and all criteria. Table 22 presents the increment in predictability.

TABLE 22.

Increment in Predictability of Principal Effectiveness Through Introduction of District Types

				Criteria				Mean
		TK	Rtg	Pers	Org	IP	Task	Increment
District Type	1	21	40	50	49	50	50	43
	2	13	10	17	26	03	22	15
	3	44	40	40	49	48	46	45
Mean Increment		26	30	36	41	34	39	34

In summary, the average multiple correlation for all principals taken together is .45. If analyzed by districts, the multiple correlation for the three district types becomes respectively, .88, .60, and .90, an average increment of predictability of .34. This is a startlingly large improvement and gives strong support to the hypothesis that different types of districts require different types of administrators.

This result is corroborated by data from the superintendents' ratings. Since the numbers are small, the ratings of superintendents made by board members and by staff members were combined. This yielded a total of 77 superintendents rated by a board member and/or a staff member. The regression for all 77 was compared with the breakdown by district type to acquire data comparable to that just presented. Unfortunately only District Type 2 had enough cases to make the

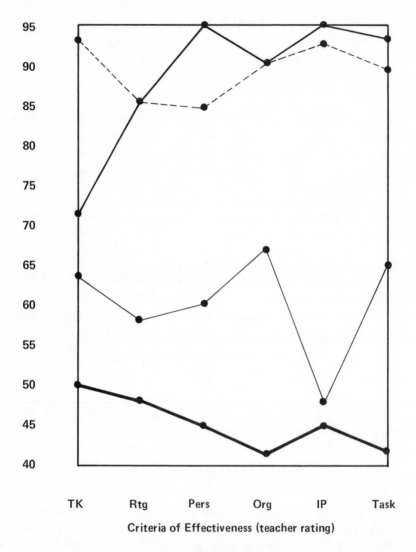

FIGURE 1.

Increment in Predictive Power (Multiple Correlation) Through
Introduction of District Type for Principals (N = 147)

LEGEND

●━━━● = Total (N = 147)
●───● = Dist. 1 (N = 35)
●───● = Dist. 2 (N = 61)
●---● = Dist. 3 (N = 36)

regression analysis meaningful, but this comparison supported the finding of the principal.

Table 23 presents the multiple correlations and adjusted multiple correlations for district type two for superintendents.

The difference in predictive power is displayed graphically in Figure 2.

The predictive improvement is given in Table 24.

TABLE 23.

Multiple Correlations and Adjusted Multiple Correlations (Lower Bound) for District Type 2 for Superintendents

	Criteria									
	Prb	Ldr	Org	Res	Com	Int	Rsp	Lik	Brd	Mean
Multiple Correlation	97	96	98	97	93	91	97	97	88	95
Adjusted Correlation	80	64	82	76	12	00	77	75	00	52

TABLE 24.

Increment in Predictability for Superintendents Due to Controlling for District Type for District Type 2

Criterion	Increment
TK	34
Rtg	32
Res	38
Prb	31
Com	45
Ldr	48
Brd	27
Mnt	28
Org	36
Mean	35

This result (mean increment = .35) is almost identical to the increment in predictability reported for principals (.34).

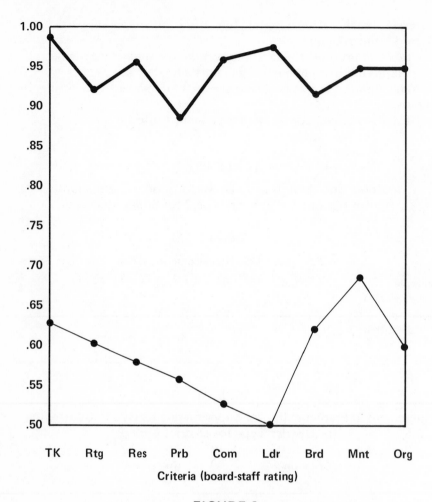

FIGURE 2.

Increment in Predictive Power Through Introduction
of District Type for Superintendents (N = 77)

Criteria (board-staff rating)   Multiple Correlation (Unadjusted)

LEGEND
●━━━● = District 2 (N = 77)
●───● = Total (N = 95)

The hypothesis that administrators function differently in different types of districts is confirmed. Prediction of administrative success is improved by about .34 if district type is taken into account.

The overall result, combining all principals and superintendents together, district types together, and combined criteria, is that administrative success overall is predicted by the predictor variables .64. When district types are introduced, prediction increases to .85.

After the extensive theoretical development of the variables, we can now assess the contribution each made to the prediction of administrative effectiveness. Detailed results will be presented, including analysis of the specific performance of each predictor variable, discussion of the type of administrator successful in each district type, and results of testing FIRO hypotheses.

EVALUATION OF INDIVIDUAL VARIABLES

LIPHE

Factor analysis reduced the LIPHE scales to two factors, dissatisfaction with mother and dissatisfaction with father. Two other LIPHE scales were added to the analysis because of their unique contribution: "When I was a child, I wanted my father to allow me more freedom" and "When I was a child, my father wanted me to be a better person."

Administrators dissatisfied in their early relations with their fathers tended to give interactors the impression of not respecting or liking them. This could certainly be a case of transference, passing on to interactors—who perceived the feelings accurately—the dissatisfaction felt for a father.

This result was true for both superintendents and principals, and especially true for superintendents from school districts located in population centers (District Type 2). In this district type, satisfaction with the relation with father was a strong positive factor in administrative success, especially as judged by the criteria of organizational ability, problem-solving ability, ability to use human resources, educational leadership, and relations with the school board.

In general, satisfaction with the childhood relation with the father was a strong positive indicator of administrative success especially for superintendents. The trait was also positive for both superintendents and principals for interpersonal effectiveness.

Administrators who felt dissatisfied with their early relations with their mothers have almost the opposite pattern from those who felt dissatisfied with their fathers. Superintendents with this trait do quite well in making their subordinates feel accepted, and so do principals in small districts (Type 3). Small-town principals who are dissatisfied with their childhood relations with their mothers are also rated high overall.

Superintendents who were not satisfied with their relations with their mothers in the population center districts (Type 2) do extremely well on organizational ability, ability to use human resources, problem-solving ability, educational leadership, and relations with board members.

Administrators with a satisfactory relationship with their fathers but not with their mothers tend to make their subordinates feel significant, competent, and liked. In addition, if they are superintendents in a population center district, they will be very successful by every criterion. The mechanism of identification may account for some of these roles.

Administrators who, as children, wanted their fathers to allow more freedom are generally unsuccessful as superintendents in a population-center district. However, subordinates do not feel as unaccepted as do those under an administrator who is dissatisfied in general with his relations with his father.

Administrators who felt that their fathers were generally dissatisfied with them do very well as principals in suburban communities (District Type 1), rating well overall and on personal, organizational, and interpersonal factors. However, if they are superintendents in population-center districts they are quite unsuccessful on personal and organizational task factors and on eliciting from staff and board members feelings that they are significant and competent.

For male administrators, who comprised the large majority, this finding suggests that perhaps a dissatisfied father acts as a motivator to his son. In a suburban area a highly motivated administrator fits into the general suburban conception of a go-getting, ambitious man. But in a population-center area this trait may be perceived as pushy and over-eager, and be regarded as disharmonious with the values of such a community.

FIRO-F

The six FIRO-F scales were reduced to two by the factor analysis. One factor comprised all expressed scales for inclusion, control, and affection. The other factor comprised wanted scales for the same dimensions.

1. An administrator who wants people to feel that he is significant, competent, and likeable is successful on organizational factors as a principal in a small district (Type 3) and does well as a superintendent

in population-center districts (Type 2). As a small-district principal, he is especially strong on the use of human resources and on educational leadership, although he is undistinguished on interpersonal factors and overall rating. As a population-center superintendent he rates especially high on the use of human resources, communication, problem-solving ability, organizational competence, and ability to deal with the school board.

2. An administrator who feels that people are important, competent, and likeable does poorly as a principal in a suburban district (Type 1) especially with regard to task abilities. As a superintendent, this type of person does poorly in general. His overall rating is very low, especially in the judgment of his staff members. Task ability is low, as is his ability to deal effectively with board members.

Sophisticated suburbanites seem to look down on administrators who profess much liking and respect for people generally. Perhaps this attitude is seen as insincere because staff members, the people who know the superintendent best, are especially negative toward administrators manifesting this trait. On the other hand, the desire to be liked seems to be a very attractive trait to people in small communities and population centers. Perhaps it is a homely virtue, in keeping with the mores of such communities. Stereotypes of suburbia and small town were supported by this finding.

COPE

The five measures of preferred defense mechanisms were reduced by factor analysis to Denial and Projection.

1. An administrator who uses projection as a preferred defense does very badly as a principal in a suburban district. He does poorly on task factors and on his ability to transmit feelings of acceptance to his teachers. The same is true, but to a lesser degree, when such an administrator is a principal in a very small district (Type 3) and in a moderate district (Type 5). As a superintendent, this type of person does fairly well in general, but very badly in a population-center district, particularly as judged by his ability in problem solving, organizing, and using human resources.

2. An administrator who, as a method of defense, tends to deny anxiety does very well as a small-district principal or as a superintendent in a population-center district. However, this type of administrator does poorly as principal in a population-center district on the various criteria of task performance, but better as superintendent on the interpersonal qualities.

Projection has been found to be a very hostile defense; in the extreme it becomes paranoia. Cohen (1956), for example, found that two projectors together had the most hostile interaction of any combination of defenders. The picture on denial is much more mixed. Deniers often give the appearance of competence, since nothing ever seems to ruffle them. On the other hand, they sometimes fail to recognize problems and their importance.

It appears that the hostility behind the projective defense is sensed by the administrator's interactors and reacted to negatively. Variation in outcome of the use of denial leads to an unclear picture of the relation of the defense to administrative performance.

VAL-ED

Factor analysis divided VAL-ED scales from each other more than it did those of the other tests, and combined them with scales from other instruments. Four factors emerged that were composed largely of VAL-ED scales.

1. A principal who feels that a school should encourage close, personal relations among administrators, teachers, and students does well in a suburban district, but very poorly in a small-community district. There is a strong tendency for a small district to reject this attitude. This view is especially related to the failure of such an administrator to elicit from teachers confidence that the administrator feels they are significant, competent, and likeable. This trait is not related to superintendent success.

2. A superintendent who feels that education is important in itself and not just as an employment aid will be exceptionally successful in all phases of administration in a suburban district, but will not do well in a population-center district, although the failure will not be as great as a success in the suburban superintendency.

3. Administrators who conform to the dominant wishes of those above them do well as suburban principals but poorly as superintendents and, to a lesser extent, do poorly as population-center principals. Their performances as population-center superintendents are mixed. They do badly on problem solving, organization, use of human resources, communication, and board relations. But they do well on educational leadership and having teachers feel they are liked by the administrators. As superintendents, they do poorly overall.

4. Principals who believe that teachers should regulate classrooms strictly do well in a small-school district, but poorly in a suburban district and in a medium-size area. They are very successful as superintendents, especially as seen by staff.

Small-town principals succeed more if they take an impersonal, task-oriented attitude about the educational situation, while successful suburban principals prefer a more personal, less disciplinary relationship in the school. This may reflect the greater psychological sophistication of suburbia, where a more permissive educational philosophy must be espoused. Old-fashioned values, like strict regulation of the classroom and impersonal relations among children, teachers, and administrators in which everyone "keeps his place," characterize small-town school districts. Superintendents seem to be able to hold, successfully, values supporting nonconformity more easily than principals.

Intelligence

Administrators who rate high on intelligence do very well on technical knowledge both as principals and as superintendents. In a suburban principalship, they do not give teachers a feeling of acceptance. In a medium-size district (Type 5), they do fairly well in general. However, the oustanding, and by far the clearest, characteristic of highly intelligent administrators is their knowledge of educational administration. This is an important finding.

Intelligence and technical knowledge are closely related to each other and have little relation to any other criterion of successful administration. Since most training for educational administration concentrates heavily on transmitting intellectual material (except for intern programs), failure to relate mastery of this information to other criteria of successful administration suggests a re-evaluation of training.

Conservatism

Administrators who are conservative in political outlook and educational values do very poorly as superintendents, as judged by both staff and board members. They also do not do well as principals in either suburban or population-center districts. As superintendents in a population-center district, they also do poorly in general, with an interesting exception—they do give teachers the feeling that they think teachers are significant, competent, and liked.

In political orientation, board members are most conservative, teachers are most liberal, and superintendents and staff members are in-between. Within the range of this middle-of-the-road philosophy, administrators who tend toward the liberal side have more success. This is true for superintendents as rated by both staff and board members, even though board members tend to be more conservative.

Successful superintendents have a tendency to be more nonconformist than less successful ones.

Family Pattern

Administrators who come from large families do very well as principals in a suburban or small district, but not very well in a population center or in a moderate district. In general, they are successful superintendents except in population-center districts, where they do quite badly overall.

Administrators who are earlier born tend to be successful small-district or suburban principals. They are also successful as superintendents, except in population-center districts where they are rated as poor on task abilities but fairly good on the interpersonal aspects of administration.

One of the original hypotheses of this study is partially confirmed by this finding. The older child in a large family is a more successful principal in both suburban and small districts and a more successful superintendent in general. However, in population-center districts, administrators from small families seem to do better. The reasons for this are not clear.

Job Characteristics

An administrator with many years of teaching experience is outstandingly unsuccessful both as principal and as superintendent. Although this was true for every type of district, it was especially true for principals in suburban and medium-size districts, for population-center superintendents, and for superintendents as judged by their staff. This variable was more negatively related to administrative effectiveness than any other predictor variable in the battery.

Administrators who have held positions for a long time do well in task performance as population-center superintendents though not as well interpersonally. They do very poorly on all aspects of administration as suburban principals.

Administrators whose major teaching field was in a scientific area do well as principals in a medium-size district. However, they do poorly in a suburban principalship in the interpersonal area and in small-community principalships generally.

These results have many important implications. The surprising result that the longer an administrator has been a teacher, the less effective is his administrative skill is remarkably consistent over principalships and superintendencies for all types of districts. This finding contradicts the beliefs that govern training programs and legal re-

quirements for administrative credentials, although it has appeared in some research studies (Griffiths, 1956, 1959). Teaching and administration require different qualities, or at least they develop different qualities in their practitioners. Also, too many years in the teaching role may develop an identification that is difficult to alter when the role changes. Administrators who go directly into administration may have a greater interest in that field and may have been specially selected for their administrative potential.

Sex

A female administrator is highly regarded as a superintendent by her staff. She also does well on the technical side as a suburban principal, but not quite so well in making teachers feel that she respects and likes them.

It is very likely that because it is so much more difficult for a woman to be selected as an administrator, any woman who succeeds in achieving that position is more carefully selected and is, on the whole, more capable than the average male administrator.

Marriage

An administrator who is married does very well as a small-district principal, especially in the interpersonal area. Stated in the opposite way, unmarried principals do not succeed in small towns. However, they do quite well as suburban principals, especially in personal and organizational abilities. Married superintendents in population centers are rated quite well in all phases of their job.

This result confirms an earlier one supporting the stereotype of the small-town district as adhering to the more traditional, conservative values and the suburban district having a more sophisticated value system. In this case, the stability of being married is an important factor for small-town administrative success, while unmarried administrators may function well in a suburban area.

Religion

Administrators who prefer a religion with a high social status (i.e., Episcopal) are rated as good technical administrators as small-district principals. Their overall rating and personal and organizational abilities are well thought of. Here, too, it is more revealing to state this finding in the other direction. Members of low-status religions (none, agnostic, Jewish, Catholic) do not succeed as small-community principals. They do very well, however, as superintendents when rated by their staff members.

The conservatism of the small town is again supported in the area of religion. The contact theory of prejudice is supported by the fact that staff members, who know superintendents best, rate those with low-status religions very high. (The contact theory states that prejudice is much less in people who have intimate contact with the group that is the target of prejudice.)

Social Status

Administrators who are well-established citizens in terms of income, mobility, and age are generally very low on technical knowledge of administration. They succeed best as suburban principals. They also do well as superintendents as seen by their staff, except for interpersonal abilities, where they are undistinguished.

Father

Having a high-status father does not seem to be related strongly to any administrative pattern of success. This item could be omitted from the individual measures.

EVALUATION OF SITUATIONAL VARIABLES

Suburban-District Principals

(District Type 1, N = 35.) Suburban principals were very well predicted by the variables used in this study. The regression correlations predicting technical knowledge, overall rating, task performance, and interpersonal competence, were, respectively, .71, .87, .93, .95, with a mean of .87.

Principals with most technical knowledge tend to be intelligent, younger, less well established, slightly conservative, and to have been a principal a fairly long time. They are even more successful if they are female.

Best overall ratings from teachers are given to administrators with little teaching experience who are unmarried and well established, are older children from a large family where the father allowed enough freedom but was not fully satisfied with his children. These administrators feel that teachers should not regulate classroom behavior too strictly and that education is of intrinsic significance beyond its educational use.

Suburban principals judged best on ability to carry out main functions such as school maintenance, educational leadership, and the use of human resources are those with relatively little teaching experience, are earlier born in a large family with a dissatisfied father, are unmarried, well established, and feel strongly that education is important. In addition, they tend to feel more comfortable in highly structured situations and to be somewhat conformist. They do not project their feelings onto others. Females who have not been on the job very long tend to do better than their male counterparts.

The pattern of suburban principals who give teachers the feeling that the teachers are significant, competent, and likeable have many similarities to the pattern of the task-successful principal. They have taught very little, are established citizens who feel that education is important and that their fathers were not satisfied with them and they do not project their feelings onto others. Beyond this, the pattern diverges considerably. These suburban principals tend not to have high intelligence, not to have taught in a nonscientific field, and not to have a high-status father. They prefer a high-status religion, have liberal political leanings and school values, and are satisfied with their fathers in general, although they wanted their fathers to allow them more freedom.

Although the general picture of the successful suburban principal is of a young, modern, ambitious individual, there are interesting differences among the various criteria of effectiveness. The principal who is successful in engendering good feelings in his staff tends to be more easygoing and nonintellectual than the principal who is successful in his task functions.

Population-Center District Principals

(District Type 2, N = 61.) Prediction for this type of principal was good but was relatively the poorest of all the district principalships. The respective multiple correlations with technical knowledge, overall rating, task ability, and interpersonal competence were .63, .57, .65 and .48, with a mean of .58.

High overall ratings were given to principals who are established citizens, but not conservative and not conformist, and who want others to think well of them. They have had relatively little teaching experience and were earlier born children who wanted more freedom from a father who tended to be not altogether satisfied with them.

Teachers rate high on task performance principals who are politically and educationally liberal, not conformist, well-established citizens who did not teach very much, and do not deny their feelings. They also feel that their fathers would have liked them to be somewhat better than they were.

Interpersonal success was very poorly predicted for this sort of principal. There did not seem to be a clear-cut personality pattern among those rated high. Only the trait of coming from a small family where the father was somewhat dissatisfied with his children approached significance.

Small-District Principals

(District Type 3, N = 36.) Success as a small-district principal was predicted extremely well. Multiple regression scores for technical knowledge, overall rating, task efficiency and interpersonal competence were, respectively, .94, .87, .89, and .93 with a mean of .91.

Technical knowledge is greatest for principals who are intelligent, unmarried males, who do not deny their feelings, and who claim that they are not particularly disturbed if people do not think well of them. They feel that teachers should not regulate classrooms strictly. They feel that their fathers allowed them enough freedom but were not altogether satisfied with them.

High overall ratings were given to principals who are married, are older children in large families with a high-status religion, and were not satisfied with their relations with their mother. They do not believe that close personal relations should be encouraged in the school setting, and their teaching field tends toward the sciences.

Task-ability success is more frequent for principals who are married, come from a large family, tend to deny anxious feelings, want people to think well of them, think teachers should regulate the classroom strictly, and have taught in nonscience fields.

Interpersonal effectiveness is achieved best by principals who are married, come from a relatively small family with a high-status father who allowed enough freedom, were dissatisfied with their relations with their mothers, and deny anxious feelings.

Successful, small-district principals are "proper." They do what they should, come from a large family, get married, keep their proper place, adhere to one of the more acceptable religions, and do not admit to problems. They are not "complainers." This contrasts considerably with successful suburban or population-center principals who tend to be relatively more liberal and nonconformist (though not necessarily complainers).

Moderate-District Principals

(District Type 5, N = 11.) Unfortunately there were too few cases to do a regression analysis or to compute stable correlations to warrant a full discussion.

Superintendents

In general, superintendent performance was very well predicted from the variables used in the study, averaging about 13 correlation points higher than principal prediction (.59 to .46). Because the smaller number of superintendents did not allow for a factor analysis of the criteria, many more single measures of effectiveness were used. Unfortunately, in the breakdown by district type, only the population center type (Type 3) had enough cases (29) to do a regression analysis.

The superintendents were analyzed as a total group (N = 77) and as two subgroups, those rated by board members (N = 71) and those rated by members of the superintendent's staff (N = 46). There was some overlap of superintendents who were rated by both. It was hypothesized that board and staff members may prefer different qualities in a superintendent. In terms of predictability, the superintendents as rated by staff had an average multiple correlation over all criteria of .81, while the superintendents as rated by board members averaged .60. In the following discussion, it is important to keep in mind that there was, at most, only one female superintendent.

Population-Center District Superintendents

(District Type 2, N = 29.) These superintendents were predicted exceptionally well by the variables used. The mean multiple correlation for all criteria was .95.

The analysis was simplified by combining all criteria into two: task (problem-solving ability, educational leadership, organizational ability, ability to use human resources, and communication ability) and interpersonal (ability to make staff feel significant, competent, and likeable).

Superintendents rated effective on task performance are dissatisfied with the childhood relation to mother, satisfied with the relation to father, and feel that their fathers were satisfied with them as children. They tend to deny anxiety, to state that they do not care whether people think well of them or not, and to be married.

Superintendents who rate high on interpersonal effectiveness are also married, deniers, and satisfied with their fathers but not with their mothers. They feel that education is primarily aimed at preparing for occupations and practical pursuits rather than being intrinsically valuable.

This is a very interesting pattern. Apparently the clear identification with the father and not the mother is an important dynamic in the success of this superintendent. (Recall that this population was almost totally male.) In many ways he must perform in a very masculine

manner. He initiates action, shows appropriate aggression, has com-
passion, serves as a masculine model, makes decisions. If the sex
identification is feminine or conflicted, these functions could well
suffer considerably. The clarity of this result suggests that further
work on the hypothesis of relational continuity as related to adminis-
tration would be very fruitful.

Superintendents Rated by Staff Members

Staff members' ratings of superintendents were very well predicted by
the predictor variables. Overall rating was predicted with a multiple
correlation of .84. The multiple correlations for the task-performance
criteria were: use of human resources, .80; problem solving, .77;
communication, .78; educational leadership, .84; school board relations, .92; school maintenance, .79; and organizational ability, .77. The
mean predictability of the task criteria was .81.

The superintendent rated high overall by his staff members is not
conservative or conformist; does not particularly notice, respect, and
like others generally; feels that education is important for its own
sake; and has a low-status religion. A superintendent high on task
effectiveness also is nonconservative and nonconformist, but wants
other people to think well of him, is an established citizen, and feels
that a teacher should strictly regulate the classroom.

Superintendents Rated by Board Members

Prediction of administrative success as measured by board members'
ratings was good but did not reach the level of prediction of the staff-
rated superintendents. On overall rating the multiple correlation was
.60. On the task criteria the multiple correlations were: use of human
resources, .63; problem solving, .58; communications, .59; educational
leadership, .59; board relations, .61; school maintenance, .49; and organizational stability, .48. Mean for the task criteria was .51. For the
interpersonal criteria, prediction was somewhat higher: making board
members feel important, .63; making them feel competent, .64; and
making them feel liked, .62.

A superintendent rated good overall by board members is early-
born, from a large family, is quite satisfied with his relation to his
father, and wants people to think well of him. He is not conservative in
his views, especially political, and is not among the more intelligent
superintendents.

A superintendent rated high on task performance also is early
born from a large family and wants people to think well of him. He
tends to be a conformist.

A superintendent who has successful interpersonal relations with school board members has a high-status father with whom his relations were quite satisfactory, but his relations with his mother were not so satisfying. He does not believe in close relations among people in the school situation. He is married, tends to deny feelings of anxiety, is somewhat conformist, and used to teach in a scientific field.

Combined Superintendents

(N = 77.) Superintendents taken as a whole, combining the ratings of both staff and board members, were predicted well. The multiple correlation for overall rating was .61. The task-performance ratings were predicted as follows: use of human resources, .58; problem solving, .57; communication, .52; educational leadership, .50; board relations, .64; school maintenance, .69; and organization, .61; with a mean on task performance of .59.

Superintendents high on an overall rating do not form a clear-cut type. They tend not to like close relations in school and they have not held their positions very long, but these are the only traits that characterized these superintendents.

A superintendent rated high on a composite of seven task-performance measures comes from a large family, is not conservative in his views, and has little teaching experience.

The paucity of results when the board and staff ratings are combined supports the view that these two rating groups have different criteria for administrator performance. If the rating groups are taken separately, a fairly clear picture emerges of superintendents selected by each group, and these pictures differ in plausible ways from each other. However, combining the two types of ratings befogs the outline of the desirable superintendent because board members and staff members apparently require different qualities.

In general the superintendents are less conservative and conformist than principals. It is difficult to tell whether administrators with these traits tend to rise to the position of superintendent or whether the job affords an opportunity to be more liberal.

CHAPTER 15

SUMMARY AND CONCLUSIONS

The aims of this study were threefold (see Chapter 1). The practical aim, "devising a satisfactory method of selecting and placing school administrators and of diagnosing administrative problems," was accomplished. Appendix A presents a detailed procedure. As a manual, it is suitable for use by any school district, school, or superintendent if it is kept up-to-date and adapted to other geographical areas by means indicated within the manual and this book. Cross-valuation studies in other areas at other times will strengthen the findings. The extremely high correlations obtained in the study support an optimistic view of the value of this manual.

The second aim of extending and testing FIRO theory and of developing more scales based on the theory was also accomplished. In fact, the extension of the theory went far beyond our initial anticipation. As the project progressed, it became clear that more and more areas would have to be covered, requiring more and more expansion of theory and measurement. Developed or refined for this project were *COPE*, *LIPHE, VAL-ED*, the *Administrator Evaluation* scales, and the non-FIRO *Certainty* and *Imagination* scales.

FIRO theory provided the framework for devising a theory and criteria for administrative effectiveness, especially in the interpersonal area, and for selecting the measures of individuals. The FIRO *hypothesis of interpersonal needs* contributed the dimensions used throughout and was in turn confirmed by the positive results and validated by the usefulness of the outcome of the study.

The *hypothesis of relational continuity* likewise suggested an area of investigation, childhood relations, and was, in turn, confirmed by the large number of positive relations explicable through the mechanisms of transference, identification, and elicitation. The formulation of this hypothesis (originally presented in Schutz, 1958, 1966) was refined in the course of the study.

The *hypothesis of compatibility* helped to organize a large part of the interpersonal aspect of the study. The principle was confirmed in general, although the gross analyses, such as that derived from factor analysis, did not allow for a more refined exploration of the hypothesis compatibility development. Perhaps future studies will remedy this.

In brief, the study succeeded admirably in expanding and refining FIRO theory and instrumentation and was, in turn, organized largely by the theory. The interweaving of theory and experiment was of great mutual benefit.

The methodological aim, to combine psychological and sociological factors on the same subjects, was also highly successful. The increase of predictability of .34, due to adding sociological dimensions, was truly surprising.

Although the results far exceeded our hopes and, at times, were quite unexpected and exciting, the study raised several unresolved issues. Discussion of these may help to point the way for building on the present work.

SAMPLE SIZE

Despite the fact that the number of people tested is very large (5,847), the actual number of administrators was not sufficient to make as many statistical breakdowns as we desired. More superintendents and principals from District Types 4 and 5 would have allowed for a more detailed analysis. The number of variables compared to number of subjects reduced the adjusted multiple correlation, which, in turn, reduces the stability of these results. Fortunately, for most results, the correlation was so high that even the adjusted figure was impressive.

Now that the preliminary work on the test battery and the method of district classification have been accomplished, more time is available for researchers to do the work necessary to increase sample size.

METROPOLITAN DISTRICTS

Unfortunately, metropolitan school districts were not well studied in this project. The reasons for this are several. There are very few such districts to begin with, only seven falling into District Type 4. Of those, only two agreed to participate in the study. One of the two would not allow teachers to be tested, which meant that since there could be no effectiveness ratings, principals could not be studied. Hence, no meaningful study was made of metropolitan districts.

The small number of metropolitan districts makes it imperative that they be studied across state lines. There just are not enough metropolises in one state. Another approach would be to consider the very large district as an entity in itself. Los Angeles, for example, for administrative purposes has divided itself into sections with associate superintendents given a great deal of autonomy for their section. The same is true of New York and of other large districts. This organization is in reality a school system in itself and is often larger than systems covering an entire state.

BEHAVIOR MEASURES

Looking over the battery of individual measures that emerged from the study, two impressions result. The battery is very comprehensive, covering a wide range of important individual traits. Virtually every measure gave excellent prediction for some important aspect of administration. Two areas, however, seem to have been neglected and probably would have enhanced the findings—interpersonal behavior and relations between the administrator's father and mother.

When the final battery was being reduced to its final form a decision was made to retain interpersonal feelings (FIRO-F, feelings) as an individual variable and to omit interpersonal behavior (FIRO-B, behavior). Space and time considerations were the main determinants of this decision. Hindsight indicates that retaining FIRO-B as well as FIRO-F would have enhanced the picture. Factors measured by FIRO-B, such as dominance, desire for closeness, and need to be with people are, obviously, important administrative traits.

In the pilot study, one of the most effective predictors of principals' performance was their perception of the relation between mother and father. This mechanism, called vicarious identification or vicarious transference, means that administrators relate to others the way their fathers related to their mothers, or the way their mothers related to their fathers. In light of the exceptional success of the LIPHE scales in the study, it seems likely that the vicarious scales would have been very revealing.

METHOD OF ANALYSIS

The large number of variables used in the study dictated the use of large data-reduction techniques such as factor analysis and multiple regression. As powerful and effective as these methods are, they lead to imprecision as the problem becomes more defined. Perhaps, now that the problem has become more focused, other statistical methods, in particular the survey techniques developed by Lazarsfeld (1956),

Hyman (1955), and Guttman (1954), may be more appropriate for investigating with more precision the relations among the variables isolated.

GENERALIZATION OF FINDINGS

When making use of the findings of this study, it is wise to stay aware of their approximate nature. District types comprise only relatively homogeneous districts, and the selection and placement method yields only a probability of success. As with any empirical study, the present results only help to reduce error. They are best used in combination with a technique that utilizes the wisdom and experience of the people making the practical decisions.

This study was done in California in the early 1960's. The results, obviously, are most applicable to that time and place. Educational situations change through time and vary geographically. The more removed in time and space from the original study, the less certainty there is that the results are applicable.

A closer look, however, reveals that many of the variables, measures, hypotheses, relationships, and findings are probably quite constant. Personality measures, criteria of effectiveness, and measures of social status, for example, are not likely to vary over time and place. Similarly, the relations found in the study appear to be stable. For example, the positive relation between an administrator's identification with father and not with mother and the administrator's task effectiveness is probably a finding that transcends setting and time, at least for several generations until the culture makes a radical change.

On the other hand, several aspects of the study are most ephemeral, and readers who wish to apply the results to their situation or to replicate the research should be aware of these. Census data changes with each census, and the composition of districts is highly influenced by the march of history. Certainly the racial strife and busing controversy, only imminent in the early sixties, has altered the demographic pattern of "percent white" and the distribution of income. In one item on political preference, political reference figures must be changed to have an accurate picture of the political leanings of a district. The relevance of student revolutions and teachers' strikes to this study is less clear and would have to be investigated empirically.

Women's liberation has already had a far-reaching impact on the study. Perhaps more than any other time factor, the advent of more women administrators, has had a change on the internal nature of administrative relations, and a follow-up to this study should certainly highlight the effect of women's increased influence on administrative relations.

Geographical differences must also be investigated empirically. Will southern or midwestern or northeastern states show the same relations within school administration as does California? Certainly, social atmospheres vary, as do traditions, values, and attitudes toward education. But do these affect the fundamental connections between the personality of administrators, the setting they are in, and their effectiveness?

TRAINING PROGRAM

In the traditional educational administration curriculum, emphasis is misplaced. Although some schools are beginning to change, the characteristic course load emphasizes technical knowledge, that is, school law, finance, organization, building, and so on. While this knowledge is obviously essential, its mastery seems to have little relation to administrative success. A small portion of the administrator's efforts involve these factors while these courses occupy a high proportion of training time. On the other hand, several areas that occupy a very large portion of administrator time are given relatively little attention in the curriculum. Consideration of criteria of administrative effectiveness and observations and interviews with many administrators suggest that the following areas of administrator training could be expanded profitably.

Human Relations

Repeatedly, administrators state that the great majority of their time is spent in dealing with people—school board members, staff, teachers, parents, community leaders, students—and that, rarely, have they had specific training in this area. At the same time, training in human relations has been developing rapidly in the past three decades. This training has evolved through lectures, demonstrations, case discussions, role playing, T-groups, sensitivity training, and the encounter group. Growth and development of these methods for exploring interpersonal relations has been very rapid and, though sometimes highly controversial, encounter groups have become established as an important tool in schools, industry, religion, and many other aspects of the culture (see Schutz, 1975). The encounter method is based on increasing awareness, finding what is true and expressing it honestly, and taking responsibility for one's own behavior and feelings. The technique involves having administrative trainees form a group of their own and express their feelings about the group, about each other, and about themselves. This gives them an opportunity to understand group processes better, to know the impact they make on others, and to understand themselves more. Where it has been tried, the method seems to be very effective as a technique for training in a field in which it is traditionally very difficult to provide a long-lasting learning experience. To use the experience best, encounter should be offered early in the training program.

Scientific Method

Administration is, by definition, a decision-making function. Yet training in scientific method is not always a central part of the administrative curriculum. Administrators need specific training in formulating problems, gathering and evaluating evidence, and testing hypotheses. Coursework in which the general principles of scientific method are taught and their application to administration are demonstrated through such topics as sampling community attitudes, evaluating research reports, and initiating needed research would greatly strengthen the training program for administrators.

Teaching Requirement

The lengthy teaching requirement (five years in California, for example) for a credential in educational administration seems not only unnecessary but is actually a deterrent to obtaining effective administrators. Consistently, the study results indicate that the longer the teaching experience, the lower the effectiveness rating of the administrator.

It is not that no teaching experience is required for administrative training. The justifiable objective of the teaching requirement is to give the administrator a thorough acquaintance with the primary function of the school, teaching. There are two difficulties with this view: (1) there are many other functions of the school with which first-hand acquaintance would also be valuable; and (2) teaching is very different at different grade levels and with different types of students. A teaching requirement that involves just length of time does not guarantee experience with teaching diversity. There is also evidence that the lengthy teaching requirement reduces the quality of the candidate for administrator. This requirement frequently has to be met prior to entry into an administrative training program. To many bright young people entering the field of administration, the anticipation of having to teach for five years before they enter graduate school discourages their entry into the field. In five years, they could receive a doctorate in another field.

To meet these objections, the teaching requirement could evolve into an expanded internship requirement such that administrative trainees are given first-hand experience with all aspects of the school. They may, for example, serve an apprenticeship in the business office, with the school psychologist, with the school nurse, with the custodial service, and with the school board during deliberations. (Some training institutions and school districts already have programs similar to this.) Trainees should also be involved in curriculum discussions and special teacher workshops, attend conventions of administrators, and, in short, participate in all the activities relevant to their future jobs. Coordinated with these activities, the trainee can teach in the primary grades, the intermediate grades, and high school (depending on the level of his administrative goal) and gain experience with intellectually gifted classes, retarded classes, heterogeneous classes, and special education classes (blind, etc.). The length of time required for the internship is whatever length of time is needed to accomplish all these activities well.

Teaching Skills and Administrative Skills

Teaching skills and administrative skills are not the same. Although some people are talented in both areas, it is much more common to find these skills existing independently. Just as most successful baseball managers tend to have been poor or mediocre players (Alston, McCarthy, Stengel), many fine administrators were undistinguished teachers.

Failure to acknowledge these differences in teaching and administrating skills has led to the situation in which a very good teacher feels obligated to become an administrator in order to "advance," that is, to make more money. Too often, the result is that the school loses a good teacher and gains an ordinary administrator.

A simple remedy for this situation is to separate the career path for administrators from that of teachers. Selection for the training program, including the internship recommended above, would begin early for administrators. Their path of advancement would be made clear, they would start on the administrative ladder at the same time as their colleagues in non-education fields. Teachers would start at a similar point, being selected for a teacher training program with a clear path of advancement. Their advancement would not be to administrative positions, for which they are not trained, but for ever more highly skilled teaching situations. They would advance to master teachers, gradually handling more challenging situations such as teaching advanced classes for bright students; teaching the retarded, and the handicapped; testing new experimental methods; developing new methods for the early grades; and perhaps, ultimately, teaching teachers.

Parallel career paths, to be meaningful, require parallel pay. As they move up their skill ladders, teachers and administrators should receive the same salary. The best teachers would receive as much money as the best administrators. Not only would this be just, but it would remove a large cause of resentment and derision that we observed in many of the school districts we visited.

At the present time, neither teaching nor administration enjoys the high status it deserves. Teaching is too often thought of as a convenient occupation for a woman until she marries. Administration is often passed off as an occupation for someone who cannot teach. In fact, both require a high degree of ability to perform well. Contaminating career paths has contributed to their disrepute. By establishing separate training programs and by focusing on the fascinating and challenging aspects of each profession, both teaching and administration may come to be recognized as the skilled arts they, indeed, are.

A PERSONAL OBSERVATION

Since the study was completed, the techniques and principles that emerged from it have come to public attention. The exposures of Watergate, the CIA, the FBI, illegal campaign contributions, and the like, have focused the public consciousness of the role of honesty in public life. Increasingly, the key role of honesty in effective human relations has become apparent. My observation of the administrative scene, enhanced by more recent experience, leads me to believe that a large percentage of administrators' problems would disappear, and a large number of administrators' energy would return, if they made honesty their policy.

Similarly, the issue of self-responsibility has been refined and clarified over the past several years (see Schutz, in press). As the doctrine that each person is responsible for himself or herself becomes more accepted, administrative relations become clarified. Working through this area may be done well in a good encounter group and, today, can help administrators even more than in the past.

appendixes

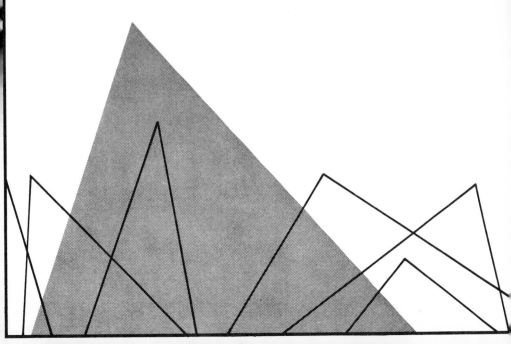

appendixes

APPENDIX A

A MANUAL FOR ADMINISTRATOR SELECTION, PLACEMENT, AND ANALYSIS

What was the point of this exercise? After all the time, energy, and money spent on this project; after all the man hours, cooperation, theory, test construction, reviews of the literature; after factor analyses, cluster analyses, multiple regressions, and Guttman scales; after facet designs, dichotomous decisions, transference, identification, affection, and percent white; after imagination and mobility, certainty and father's income, small districts and suburban; and even after the triumphant final correlations; after all of this—so what?

We set out to discover how better to select and place school administrators and how to analyze their difficulties. All of our work is for naught if we cannot shed light on this problem.

Fortunately, we can. To demonstrate how, we have composed a manual for those of you who wish to select, place, or analyze. All you need do is follow the manual.

This manual is designed for use in the following situations.

1. Selection of school superintendent
2. Selection of school principal
3. Placement of school administrator into one of two or more school districts
4. Analysis of areas of strength and of weakness for an administrator in a specific school district

Although the data used to develop this procedure were derived from the California school system of the early 1960s, the procedure for classifying districts is applicable to any school district at any place or time. At appropriate places, alterations of the data required to apply this procedure are indicated. In this manual, we present the original data as an aid in presenting the procedure and for those who feel these data may approximate their situation closely enough to be directly usable.

Students, also, may find the data useful for further explorations and research.

The method is best used as a supplement to other methods of administrative selection, placement, and analysis. Commonly used techniques, such as personal interviews or letters of recommendation, are in no sense superseded by the present procedure.

OUTLINE OF PROCEDURE

I.Describe Candidates
   A. Questionnaire
   B. Scoring

II.Classify Districts
   A. District category
   B. District type
      1. Convert district area to census units
      2. Compile census data
      3. Convert to deciles
      4. Classify district
   C. Example of district classification

III.Criteria of administrative effectiveness

IV.Example of applications of procedure
   A. Selection
   B. Placement
   C. Analysis

DESCRIBE CANDIDATES

Each administrator or candidate for administrator (the word candidate will be used to mean the person to be selected, placed, or analyzed) is assigned a score on each predictor variable. The variables used to predict administrative performance are presented in Table A.1.

Scores

For each candidate, the questionnaire is scored and a score for each predictor variable is computed. The final score for each candidate is an array of twenty-four numbers arranged in order of predictor variables.

TABLE A-1.
Predictor Variables

Name (content and positive end of scale)

1. I am dissatisfied with the way my father related to me.
2. I am dissatisfied with the way my mother related to me.
3. I want people to notice, respect, and like me.
4. I am interested in, respect, and like people.
5. I prefer conformity and conventionality.
6. People in the school situation should have close and personal relations with each other.
7. Education is of importance in developing the whole child.
8. I am conservative.
9. I handle anxiety by attributing my unacceptable feelings and motives to others.
10. I handle anxiety by denying the problem or its importance.
11. I am an established citizen.
12. I come from a large family.
13. I have a high-status father.
14. I am male.
15. I am married.
16. I prefer a high-status religion.
17. I am intelligent.
18. I was a later born child in my family.
19. The teacher should regulate classroom behavior.
20. When I was a child, I wanted my father to allow me more freedom.
21. My father wanted me to be a better person.
22. I have held my position for many years.
23. I have been a full-time teacher for many years.
24. My teaching field tended toward the sciences and mathematics.

Questionnaire

Scores on predictor variables are derived from answers to items in the appropriate questionnaire. The questionnaire is administered to all administrators or candidates for administrator involved in selection, placement, or analysis. Table A.2. presents the components of the test battery[1] and the time required for administration.

---

[1]See Appendix D for availability.

TABLE A-2.
Questionnaire Battery

Predictor Variable	Scale	Number of Items	Administration
1, 2, 20, 21	LIPHE	81	20 minutes
3, 4	FIRO-F	54	10
5, 6, 7, 8, 19	VAL-ED	81	20
	Certainty	9	1
	Imagination	9	1
	Politics	1	¼
9, 10	COPE	30	20
11	Age	1	¼
	Income	1	¼
	Stability	1	¼
12, 18	Birth Order	2	1
13	Father's Occupation	1	¼
	Father's Education	1	¼
14	Sex	1	¼
15	Marital Status	1	¼
16	Religious Preference	1	¼
17	Intelligence	37	20
22	Yrs. in position	1	¼
23	Yrs. in full time teaching	1	¼
24	Major Field	1	¼

Testing time is 60 to 120 minutes.   315   96 minutes

CLASSIFY DISTRICTS

The districts for which candidates are to be selected or within which analysis is to be made, or the districts in which a candidate is to be placed, are assigned a district category and a district type.

District Category

District categories are elementary, high school or junior high school, and unified or union. These categories vary from state to state and over time. Whichever categories prevail in your state is the proper set to use.

Assignments of weights to demographic factors (see Table A.5)

sometimes differ among district categories. This was true for the district categories of California, 1962.

For purposes of exposition of this procedure, only the unified district will be presented. Other categories follow the same format.

District Types

There are five district types that have been demonstrated to differ markedly in requirements for an administrator's success. Place your district in one of these types. They are presented in Table A.3.

TABLE A-3.
District Types

Type 1. *Suburban.* Located around large metropolitan areas such as Los Angeles and San Francisco (Culver City, Acalanes).

Type 2. *Population centers.* Somewhat removed from metropolitan areas (Stockton, Vallejo).

Type 3. *Very small.* Districts within very small communities (Middletown, Calistoga).

Type 4. *Metropolitan and large suburban.* (San Francisco, Pasadena).

Type 5. *Moderate.* Medium size districts, not near metropolitan areas (Delano, Folsom).

Classification of a district into one of these five types requires several stages.

CONVERT DISTRICT AREA TO CENSUS UNITS

Since sampling units employed by the United States Census are not typically identical with the school district boundaries, it is necessary to find census units that most closely approximate the school units. This is accomplished by placing a map of your school district over a map of the state census units and finding the set of census units best approximating the district. Each school district is converted into its equivalent census tracts or standard metropolitan statistical areas (SMSA). The following rules are used for conversion.

1. If school district covers three-fourths or more of census tract, division, or SMSA, the entire census unit is attributed to the district.

2. If between one-fourth and three-fourths of tract, division, or SMSA is covered by school district, half of total population of that census unit is attributed to school area.

3. If less than one-fourth of census tract, division or SMSA falls within school district area, that census unit is disregarded.

4. If census unit covers two school districts, half of that census unit's population figures is attributed to each school area.

COMPILE CENSUS DATA

School Enrollment Ratio (Enrl): the percentage of the total population of the district enrolled in public schools (excluding college enrollment).

Education (Educ): the median number of years of school completed for persons twenty-five years old and over.

Geographical Mobility (Mob): the number of people over five years of age who left the county, or standard metropolitan statistical area in the five-year period between 1955 and 1960 divided by the total number of people in the district who were over five years of age. (High number means high mobility.)

Personal Income (Inc): the median income of persons living in the district.

Income Variation (VInc): the semi-interquartile range (the difference, in deciles, between the income of persons at the 25th and 75th percentiles).

Occupational Level (Occ): the average level of occupation, as defined by the average score on occupations as classified by the census (Table A.4). Multiply number of persons in each census occupation by number given in Table A.4, and divide by the total number of persons in the district.

TABLE A-4.
CENSUS OCCUPATIONS AND VALUES

Professional, technical, and kindred workers	7
Manager, officers and proprietors, including farm	6
Clerical and kindred workers	3
Sales workers	3
Craftsmen, foreman, and kindred workers	4
Operatives and kindred workers	2
Private household workers	2
Service workers except private household	2
Laborers, except mine	1

Occupation Variation (VOcc): the semi-interquartile range.

Median Age (Age): take directly from the census.

Percent Married (Mar): take directly from the census.

Percent White (Wht): take directly from the census.

School (District) Size (Siz): the average daily attendance (ADA) in public schools, as supplied by the Annual Financial Report of the State Board of Education.

Tax Wealth (Wlth): the assessed valuation per ADA of school district, as published in the Annual Financial Report. For attendance areas for which there are no published figures, take the value assigned to the district in which they are located.

School Expenditures (Xpd): reported in the Annual Financial Report as current expenditures per ADA.

CONVERT TO DECILES

Convert the raw scores obtained on these variables to decile scores. Since distribution of values varies from one category of district to another, decile scores also vary. Table A.5 presents conversion charts for unified districts for each variable for California, 1962. For greater accuracy, these tables must be computed for state and year where this procedure is being applied.

TABLE A-5.

Conversion Chart of Raw Scores to Deciles for Unified School Districts (California, 1962)

Decile Score	1) School Enroll-ment ratio	2) Education (Median yrs. school)	3) Geographical Stability
0	15.2-16.8	9.1-10.2	49.6-61.1
1	16.9-17.6	10.3-10.5	46.3-49.5
2	17.7-19.4	10.6-11.3	44.6-46.2
3	19.5-21.1	11.4-11.5	43.2-44.5
4	21.2-23.1	11.6-11.8	40.3-43.1
5	23.2-24.0	11.9-12.0	37.7-40.2
6	24.1-25.0	12.1-12.1	35.2-37.6
7	25.1-26.4	12.2-12.2	32.6-35.1
8	26.5-27.8	12.3-12.4	25.7-32.5
9	27.9-28.8	12.5-13.1	20.3-25.6

TABLE A-5 (Continued).

Decile Score	4) Personal Income (Median family income)	5) Variation in Income	6) Occupation Level
0	$2766-4855	2	2.62-3.16
1	4856-5482	3	3.17-3.28
2	5483-5943	4	3.29-3.51
3	5944-6157	—	3.52-3.60
4	6158-6454	—	3.61-3.69
5	6455-6776	5	3.70-3.83
6	6777-7135	—	3.84-3.96
7	7136-7446	—	3.97-4.11
8	7447-7837	6	4.12-4.19
9	7838-8105	7	4.20-5.70

Decile Score	7) Variation in Occupational Level	8) Median Age	9) Percent Married	10) Percent White
0	2	23.3-25.0	31.3-57.3	73.6-82.3
1	—	25.1-26.9	57.4-62.8	82.4-90.3
2	3	27.0-27.9	62.9-65.6	90.4-94.6
3	—	28.0-29.8	65.7-67.2	94.7-95.6
4	—	29.9-31.5	67.3-69.1	95.7-97.0
5	4	31.6-32.9	69.2-70.8	97.1-98.5
6	—	33.0-35.5	70.9-72.2	98.6-99.0
7	—	35.6-37.6	72.3-73.2	99.1-99.2
8	5	37.7-41.4	73.3-74.1	99.3-99.4
9	6—7	41.5-47.5	74.2-81.5	99.5-99.9

Decile Score	11) School District Size (ADA)	12) Tax Wealth (AV/ADA) In Thousands	13) School Expenditures (CE/ADA)
0	19-148	15-23.44	32,099-36,322
1	158-259	23.45-26.4	36,359-38,423
2	264-388	26.5-29.1	38,500-40,022
3	390-550	29.15-32.2	40,056-41,209
4	557-816	32.3-34.4	41,793-43,919
5	817-1122	34.5-38	44,028-45,673
6	1126-1625	38.5-44	45,769-48,571
7	1663-3007	45-53	48,630-53,558
8	3021-5450	54-72	53,590-58,484
9	5678-134,324	73-327	61,955-100,279

Compare profile of decile scores for your school district with profiles of district types. Table A.6 presents these profiles.

TABLE A-6.

Decile Score Profiles for District Types
for Unified School Districts (California, 1962)

Census Variables

District Type	Enrl	Educ	Inc	VInc	VOcc	Age	Mar	Wht	Size	WIth	Xpd
1	1	6	5	6	3	7	1	1	8	7	7
2	5	7	9	5	2	5	7	7	5	4	5
3	4	4	5	3	4	3	3	2	7	2	4
4	4	2	1	6	5	8	5	6	0	8	8
5	7	1	2	2	9	3	5	5	3	3	0

Because comparisons are made on clusters or factors for unified districts, Age is counted twice and Mobility and Occupation are omitted. In other words, the average age of the inhabitants of unified districts is an important variable in assigning the district to a type, while occupation and mobility are not as discriminating. (This is not true for other district categories.)

CLASSIFY DISTRICTS

Compute average discrepancy score between your district profile and each district type. The district type with the smallest discrepancy is the district type of your district.

To estimate how well your district fits into its type, a second digit is attached to district type. If the mean decile discrepancy score is 1.2 or below, then your district is a "close" fit. Any score of 1.3 or above is "not close." "Unique fit" is defined as a difference of 1.1 or more between the mean score on the first and second best-fitting clusters. A score of 1.0 or below is considered "not unique." The second district code digit is assigned to reflect the goodness of the fit of the district to district type as follows.

TABLE A-7.

Certainty

Code	Fits District Type	Unique Fit
.1	close	unique
.2	close	not unique
.3	not close	unique
.4	not close	not unique

Your district is assigned a two-digit number indicating the district type and the goodness of fit to that type.

Example of District Classification

To make clear the procedure for district classification, a hypothetical district will be assigned values and taken through the classification procedure.

Assume that the hypothetical entity, Mycroft, is a unified school district with the following values derived from the census.

1. School enrollment ratio   19.7
2. Education   11.9
3. Geographical mobility   47.1
4. Personal income   6501
5. Income variation   4
6. Occupation level   3.61
7. Occupation variation   3
8. Median age   37.9
9. Percent married   74.3
10. Percent white   99.1
11. School district size   712
12. Tax wealth   51,178
13. School expenditures   52,733

1. These values are converted to deciles by use of Table A.5. Decile scores are, respectively: 3, 5, 8, 5, 2, 4, 2, 8, 9, 7, 4, 7, 7.

2. Deciles are compared with profiles of Unified District Types (Table A.6), making certain that mobility and occupation are omitted and that age is counted twice.

The following are mean profile differences of Mycroft from each district cluster.

Difference from:

Type 1 = 2+1+0+4+1+1(+1)+8+6+4+0+0 = 28(÷12) = 2.3
Type 2 = 2+2+4+3+0+3(+3)+2+0+1+3+2 = 25(÷12) = 2.1
Type 3 = 1+1+0+1+2+5(+5)+6+5+3+5+3 = 37(÷12) = 3.1
Type 4 = 1+3+4+4+3+0(+0)+4+1+4+1+1 = 26(÷12) = 2.2
Type 5 = 4+4+3+0+7+5(+5)+4+2+1+4+7 = 46(÷12) = 3.8

Mycroft fits best, but not well, in District Type 2 (Population Center) and not uniquely, since it fits almost as well in District Type 4

(Metropolitan). It is designated as District Type 24 (not close—not unique).

CRITERIA OF ADMINISTRATIVE EFFECTIVENESS

The decision as to which criteria of administrative effectiveness are of most importance is that of the person or group doing the selection. They must decide what they want from the administrator. The following are the criteria for principals and for superintendents.[1]

For Principal

Overall rating (Rtg); the assessment of a principal's effectiveness as compared to other principals known to the raters (the average of all ratings given by principal's teachers).

Personal traits (Pers): the qualities characteristic of a principal's personal performance, including problem-solving ability, ability to maintain the school plant, and educational leadership.

Organizational traits (Org): the ability to integrate and coordinate various elements of school situation into efficient operation, including organizational efficiency, ability to use human resources well, and skill in communication.

Interpersonal traits (Lik): satisfaction with interpersonal situation that a principal elicits from teachers, staff, and board members; the degree to which raters feel that the principal finds them important, competent, and likeable.

Task ability (Tsk): combination of personal and organizational traits; the sum of all task-ability scales used to assess administrative performance.

For Superintendent

Overall rating (Rtg): general administrative effectiveness.

Problem solving (Prb): the degree to which efficient solution of school district problems is facilitated.

Communication (Com): the degree to which an effective system of communication is maintained throughout school district.

Educational leadership: (Ldr): the degree to which a superintendent provides a high level of educational leadership.

---

[1]Administrator Evaluation Scales used to measure these criteria are given in Appendix D.

School maintenance (Mnt): the degree to which such matters as schedules, building maintenance, and availability of teaching materials are dealt with efficiently.

Organization (Org): the degree to which activities are organized to obtain maximum benefit from district resources.

Use of human resources (Res): the degree to which school personnel feel motivated, prepared, and given an opportunity to do their best for the school district.

Board relations (Brd): the degree to which a superintendent deals effectively with the school board.

Evaluation is accomplished by multiplying each candidate's predictor variable scores by appropriate weights. For principals, these weights are available for District Types 1, 2, and 3. For superintendents, they are available for all districts, for District Type 2, and for criteria as rated by board members and by staff. The weighted scores of each candidate are obtained. Table A.8 presents the computational weights.

EXAMPLE OF APPLICATIONS OF PROCEDURE

Selection

To demonstrate the selection technique, imagine a hypothetical example in which you wish to select a principal for the Mycroft Unified School District. There are four candidates: Abe, Barry, Charlie, and Donna.

1. *Describe Candidates*. Each takes the test battery. Table A.9 presents their hypothetical scores on the predictor variables.
2. *Classify District*. By the method described above, Mycroft is in District Type 2.
3. *Select Criterion*. Suppose you want a principal who will be very efficient. Select the criterion Task Ability (Tsk).
4. *Compute Scores*. Multiply scores for each of the four candidates by the weights for District Type 2 for the Task Ability criterion. Table A.10 shows that computation.

(If these were candidates for superintendent, and you wanted one who was compatible with the school board members, you would use weights from the Brd column in Table A.8, and so forth.)

Donna, with a score of 5551, is clearly the best candidate. Charlie, 5161, is next; followed by Abe, 2635, and Barry, 2591, both well below the top two.

TABLE A-8. Weights for Computing Degree of Administrative Success

Principals

Predictor Variables	District Type 1					District Type 2					District Type 3				
	Rtg	Pers	Org	Lik	Tsk	Rtg	Pers	Org	Lik	Tsk	Rtg	Pers	Org	Lik	Tsk
1	0	3	7	-11	1	-1	-3	-3	-8	-6	-1	0	-5	0	-1
2	0	-7	-12	0	-2	-2	-2	-3	-5	-5	10	6	11	11	2
3	-5	1	-6	-1	-1	9	11	9	10	20	5	20	33	-11	5
4	-3	-14	-12	-2	-3	4	-1	-1	4	-1	-1	14	12	6	3
5	5	13	15	-6	3	-9	-22	-15	-5	-36	-9	-10	-2	-2	-1
6	4	9	12	-2	2	-5	-11	-9	1	-20	-12	-8	-10	-29	-2
7	6	35	29	22	6	-5	4	1	-3	4	8	-1	0	27	0
8	-3	-20	-15	-33	-4	-12	-43	-40	-7	-83	1	-4	27	-18	2
9	-6	-32	-28	-24	-6	5	5	1	3	7	-2	-15	-12	5	-3
10	0	1	7	-3	1	-1	-6	-8	0	-14	1	13	13	10	3
11	20	42	58	48	10	17	28	32	17	61	10	-28	-15	-14	-4
12	30	56	70	-6	13	16	-24	-45	-44	-69	56	68	88	-35	16
13	11	-5	-18	29	-2	4	8	13	6	21	16	-7	-20	82	-3
14	1	110	131	-54	24	-11	42	104	28	145	49	66	72	-87	14
15	-89	-224	-192	-45	-42	-40	-36	41	77	5	92	240	259	285	50
16	-5	3	2	28	0	-4	-4	4	-6	0	52	50	31	20	8
17	0	2	2	-25	1	2	3	1	0	5	5	-9	-12	-7	-2
18	-42	-66	-89	23	-16	-42	-4	27	50	23	-112	-24	-73	49	-10
19	-23	-25	-35	-25	-6	-2	25	23	38	49	5	62	81	-6	14
20	-20	10	13	27	2	-30	-42	-36	-13	-78	4	26	14	-105	4
21	29	77	67	42	14	30	75	53	50	128	-25	-41	-62	4	-10
*22	-15	-25	-44	-31	-7	7	2	-5	-14	-3	-22	11	24	6	4
23	-70	-202	-190	-189	-39	-29	-58	-49	-22	-107	16	2	-12	16	-1
24	-11	-40	-26	-50	-7	22	7	27	5	34	-21	-21	-53	-20	-8
K	1086	2706	2061	1378	477	812	2843	2499	1057	5342	-789	-430	1100	1684	-153
	(÷)				(×)					(÷)	(÷)				(×)

(×) = Score must be multiplied by ten to compare with other criteria or other district types.

(÷) = Score must be divided by ten to compare with other criteria or other district types.

* = Not used for the selection process.

K = Constant to be added to each total score.

TABLE A-8 (Continued).

Predictor Variables	Superintendents — In General								District Type 2								
	Rtg	Res	Prb	Com	Ldr	Brd	Mnt	Org	Prb	Com	Ldr	Brd	Mnt	Org	Int	Resp	Lik
1	0	-4	-8	-3	-1	1	5	7	-2	-2	-10	-18	-1	-2	-8	-14	-10
2	1	3	1	0	-1	-2	-6	-5	2	3	20	22	3	3	9	14	6
3	-1	10	5	7	5	5	-3	1	4	5	13	28	4	3	18	12	-5
4	9	2	-4	-1	-4	-4	-2	-3	-2	-3	-23	-24	-2	-3	-16	-14	-6
5	6	3	2	2	-3	-11	-7	-8	-2	-2	9	-11	-1	-2	4	-1	8
6	-12	-3	2	-3	-3	4	7	4	0	-1	-9	3	-4	-3	-10	1	4
7	-11	-5	-4	2	1	4	7	5	-4	-4	2	-13	-9	-2	-25	-24	-14
8	-2	-11	-10	-11	-13	-4	-15	-9	-3	-4	-15	-7	-2	-3	-36	31	24
9	0	-7	4	-1	1	2	5	4	-3	-2	-8	-6	-2	-2	-2	-9	-3
10	-1	2	2	0	3	1	-2	-2	2	3	13	17	2	2	9	11	5
11	-6	12	9	-1	-1	11	15	10	2	4	19	36	4	4	12	16	1
12	-9	15	11	5	3	19	28	21	-11	-10	-39	-45	-5	-10	-10	-53	-15
13	7	-2	-2	3	3	-2	-4	-20	2	2	12	11	1	2	-7	13	-1
14	3	23	-22	15	18	-5	6	79	-88	-45	85	248	4	-7	-726	-164	-202
15	39	-9	33	43	18	-39	-48	-30	22	29	98	175	22	16	187	131	24
16	2	1	2	10	-3	-12	-21	-13	6	0	-6	-21	1	2	11	-8	-6
17	8	2	-5	-3	-3	9	6	7	1	1	8	-8	0	0	3	-16	-16
18	-22	-41	-28	10	8	-35	-57	-36	25	23	75	87	12	19	35	147	54
19	-20	2	0	-6	-9	20	24	22	1	6	-2	32	3	0	23	7	-8
20	-6	6	-2	2	-9	6	-6	-10	6	-8	-16	-54	-11	-5	58	5	6
21	-9	-19	6	-12	-8	-1	10	6	-9	-10	-136	-43	-10	-13	-70	-59	-2
*22	-26	-3	-10	8	14	20	22	13	4	5	49	14	4	6	31	-15	-12
23	2	-23	-5	-3	-23	-10	-15	-13	-9	-8	-29	-35	-5	-7	-28	4	12
24	8	-1	-17	-5	11	-6	-12	-12	-10	-10	-54	-43	-10	-6	-82	10	33
K	552	291	345	333	687	-31	110	27	236 (x)	139 (x)	311	50	16 (x)	179 (x)	671	-42	-18

(x) = Score must be multiplied by ten to compare with other criteria or other district types.

*   = This variable not used for the selection process.

TABLE A-8 (Continued).

Superintendents

Predictor Variables	Board Rated								Staff Rated							
	Rtg	Res	Prb	Com	Ldr	Brd	Mnt	Org	Rtg	Res	Prb	Com	Ldr	Brd	Mnt	Org
1	-5	-2	3	1	-4	-6	-2	0	-1	-3	-3	4	7	-6	2	10
2	-2	-5	-6	0	4	-2	-1	0	-1	2	0	-6	-3	5	-6	-5
3	8	16	3	8	13	9	2	4	-2	11	13	6	10	14	8	8
4	-5	-7	-2	-4	-9	-1	-3	-1	-10	4	1	-6	-5	-1	6	-1
5	-5	4	8	3	5	7	10	5	-6	-6	-2	-10	-15	-16	-6	-14
6	0	1	-1	-3	0	-2	0	-10	-2	1	1	-7	2	2	-6	-4
7	-2	-7	8	0	-5	-10	1	4	11	-4	0	13	-1	-7	3	0
8	-13	1	3	-5	-6	-7	-5	-7	-10	-23	-25	-31	-16	-21	-29	-24
9	1	5	3	3	0	5	2	3	2	3	4	1	2	2	5	7
10	0	0	-2	-1	1	2	-2	-2	1	0	-3	1	1	3	-1	-1
11	6	5	-5	5	15	14	2	1	4	31	21	1	12	44	24	28
12	20	19	19	18	7	23	14	15	8	14	19	38	3	1	7	-1
13	-4	-7	-3	-6	-5	-2	1	1	7	4	0	19	10	-6	13	8
14	2	60	-35	2	113	-12	38	-12	285	139	-95	392	655	276	138	449
15	35	24	27	22	28	65	1	45	-1	-15	21	62	-5	3	42	-25
16	0	10	10	-2	2	-7	10	0	-18	-8	6	-7	-37	1	-21	-20
17	-12	-3	7	3	-9	-4	4	1	-3	1	-10	3	0	-5	3	8
18	-51	-49	-40	-71	-33	-84	-55	-59	-27	-36	7	-41	24	-61	3	-10
19	5	6	8	-7	-22	-7	-15	-13	-4	24	22	27	32	35	21	22
20	1	-8	-8	-12	-8	-1	10	4	3	6	-6	-3	-13	9	7	-12
21	19	14	5	-29	-14	10	-18	-25	-6	8	20	18	-3	-14	4	-2
*22	-6	-21	-6	-14	-8	-19	-10	-1	4	-18	-1	-7	-7	-8	8	-11
23	6	-14	-12	-3	-23	-20	-5	-13	4	-31	-31	-10	-14	-8	-21	-26
24	-1	-6	-10	6	0	3	-1	7	11	-19	-22	-3	18	-12	-21	-1
K	895 (÷)	194	-206	339	520	99	302	328	719 (÷)	124	268	-264	-15	116	144	205

(÷) = Score must be divided by ten to compare with other criteria or other district types

* = Not used for the selection process.

TABLE A-9.

Test Scores for Four Hypothetical Candidates
for Principalship of Mycroft Unified District School

Predictor Variable	Range	Abe	Barry	Charlie	Donna
1	(0-27)	7	10	24	3
2	(0-54)	24	12	7	25
3	(0-27)	21	9	5	9
4	(0-27)	24	13	17	22
5	(0-45)	38	31	11	15
6	(0-45)	15	21	26	9
7	(0-27)	11	14	25	21
8	(0-27)	22	20	8	4
9	(0-18)	12	10	2	5
10	(0-27)	10	25	11	5
11	(1-26)	20	24	12	16
12	(1-25)	18	21	3	4
13	(1-15)	13	14	6	8
14	(1-2)	1	1	1	2
15	(1-5)	5	5	1	3
16	(1-9)	8	8	2	1
17	(0-37)	26	25	34	30
18	(1-9)	3	4	1	2
19	(0-9)	8	9	1	4
20	(0-9)	2	3	8	7
21	(0-9)	2	4	8	3
22	(1-9)	7	8	2	3
23	(1-9)	7	9	2	4
24	(1-9)	3	5	9	8

TABLE A-10.

Computation of Weighted Scores for Four Hypothetical Candidates for a District Type 2 Principalship based on Criterion of Total Task Ability

Predictor Variable	District 2 Weight (from Table A-8)	Abe	Barry	Charlie	Donna
1	-6	-42	-60	-144	-18
2	-5	-120	-60	-35	-125
3	20	420	180	100	180
4	-1	-24	-13	-17	-22
5	-36	-1368	-1116	-396	-540
6	-20	-300	-420	-520	-180
7	4	44	56	100	84
8	-83	-1826	-1660	-664	-332
9	7	84	70	14	35
10	-14	-140	-350	-154	-70
11	61	1220	1464	732	976
12	-69	-1242	-1449	-207	-276
13	21	273	294	126	168
14	145	145	145	145	290
15	5	25	25	5	15
16	0	0	0	0	0
17	5	130	125	170	150
18	23	69	92	23	46
19	49	392	441	49	196
20	-78	-156	-234	-624	-546
21	128	256	512	1024	384
22	-3	-21	-24	-6	-9
23	-107	-749	-963	-214	-428
24	34	102	170	306	272
Total of Weighted Scores		-2707	-2751	-181	259
Add Constant		5342	5342	5342	5342
Final Total		2635	2591	5161	5551

(Variable 22, years in position, is omitted, since only one candidate, at most, can now occupy the position.)

Placement

Suppose you wish to place these four candidates and you have available positions in District Types 1, 2, and 3. For simplicity, suppose the criterion remains Task Ability.

Performing the same computation as above yields scores presented in Table A.11.

TABLE A-11.

Scores of Four Hypothetical Candidates for Principalship, on Task Ability Criterion, for Three District Types

District Type 1		District Type 2		District Type 3	
Charlie	761	Donna	5551	Abe	519
Donna	440	Charlie	5161	Barry	442
Barry	439	Abe	2635	Donna	48
Abe	293	Barry	2591	Charlie	-231

Charlie is clearly the best candidate for District Type 1. Donna and Barry are in the middle, and Abe is the least likely success in a District Type 1 principalship.

As noted, Donna is the leading candidate for a District Type 2 principalship with Charlie not far behind. Abe and Barry are both a long distance from those two. However, in District Type 3, Abe is the outstanding candidate. Barry is in a solid position, while Donna is far down and Charlie is an extraordinarily bad fit.

The striking differences in preference for candidates in the three districts illustrate the vital importance of considering the type of district in selecting an administrator. The fact that three different candidates would be best in three different districts demonstrates that failure to consider district type can lead to gross misplacement.

There are two small mathematical points to note in placement. In order to make scores between districts comparable, constants given in Table A.8 must always be added to the sum of weighted scores. This constant makes the totals comparable from one district to another. In assigning weights, those for some criteria were multiplied by ten for convenience. When compared with other district scores they must be divided by ten to return them to comparability. The scores for which this must be done are indicated in Table A.8.

One score for which this division must be done is the Task Ability criterion for District Type 2. In the example above, that changes the scores of the candidates in District Type 2 to: Donna 555, Charlie 516, Abe 264, and Barry 259.

Given the scores in the example, it would be reasonable to place Charlie in District Type 1 (score of 761). He also might do well in District Type 2 (516), and he should be kept far away from District Type 3 (-231). Donna should be placed in District Type 2 (555), preferably. She should do fairly well in District Type 1 (439), but not well in District Type 3 (48). Abe has an almost opposite pattern. He should certainly go to a District Type 3 principalship (519). He would apparently do a very mediocre job in District Types 2 or 1 (264, 293). Barry is harder to place since he does not have a very high score in any district. His best bet is District Type 3 (442), followed by District Type 1 (440) and District Type 2 (259).

In other words, Charlie seems headed for suburbia and away from small towns. Abe is just the opposite. Donna would head for the outlying population centers. And Barry might try the small towns and keep open the possibility of changing occupations.

Analysis

Analysis of an administrative problem is accomplished by considering the detailed weighted scores of a candidate (Table A.10). The greatest negative scores are possible points of difficulty, and the highest positive scores are sources of strength.

Using Table A.10, the following appear to be Abe's major problems in Mycroft:

1. His conservatism (predictor variable 8);
2. His conformity (variable 5);
3. The fact that he comes from a large family (variable 12);
4. His lengthy teaching experience (variable 23).

These factors are in no sense final answers to Abe's problems in Mycroft. They may be used as starting points in a discussion between Abe and his superintendent in an attempt to analyze administrative difficulties.

Analysis of Donna's performance in the administrative role leads to the following observations.

1. Being an established citizen (variable 11) is a help to her administrative success.

2. The fact that her father wanted her to be a better person (variable 21) may have given her the kind of drive required for this job.
3. Her scientific teaching field (variable 23) helps her.
4. Her main stumbling block seems to be related to the fact that she wanted her father to allow her more freedom when she was a child (variable 20).

These clues to strengths or difficulties require different degrees of inference. Being conservative or conformist is an immediate trait that can be discussed on its own merits. However, the relation between administrative performance and having wanted more freedom when one was a child is more a basis for speculation. Perhaps Donna still wants more room to maneuver on her job. These are matters that may be explored in a discussion with people relevant to Donna's administrative situation.

APPENDIX B
CHARACTERISTICS OF TOTAL SAMPLE

TABLE B-1.

Size of Sample

Board members		231
Superintendents	57	
Staff	232	
Superintendents/Principals	38	
Principals	118	
Total Administrators		445
Teachers		3750
Parents		1421
TOTAL		5847

TABLE B-2.

Sex Distribution of Sample (in percent)

	Male	Female
Board Members	83	17
Superintendents	98	02
Staff	63	37
Superintendents/Principals	82	18
Principals	82	18
Teachers	49	51
Parents	10	90
TOTAL	44	56

169

TABLE B-3.
Marital Distribution of Sample (in percent)

	Divorced	Separated	Single	Widowed	Married
Board Members	00	00	00	01	99
Superintendents	02	00	02	02	94
Staff	03	01	09	05	82
Superintendent/Principals	08	00	00	03	89
Principals	03	01	10	06	80
Teachers	05	01	19	04	71
Parents	01	01	01	02	95
TOTAL	04	01	13	04	79

Once married (divorced, separated, or widowed)	09
Never married (single)	13
Married (now married)	79

TABLE B-4.
Age Distribution of Sample (in percent)

	Under 26	26-30	31-35	36-40	41-45	46-50	51-55	56-65	Over 65	Average Age
Board Members	00	00	13	11	30	21	15	07	03	44
Superintendents	00	00	02	14	11	19	21	32	02	51
Staff	00	03	07	12	21	18	24	14	01	47
Superintendents/ Principals	00	03	14	14	23	29	09	09	00	44
Principals	00	02	14	20	20	18	14	10	01	44
Teachers	12	15	16	14	13	11	10	08	01	36
Parents	01	07	19	27	26	14	05	02	00	39
TOTAL	08	12	16	17	17	12	10	07	01	38

TABLE B-5.
Distribution of Religious Preference of Sample (in percent)

	None or Agnostic	Jew	Cath	Bap	Meth	Cong	Unit	Epis	Other
Board Members	05	03	12	08	26	01	01	11	27
Superintendents	06	00	00	06	31	13	00	07	37
Staff	04	01	08	05	25	09	02	11	35
Superintendents/ Principals	08	00	08	05	21	05	00	16	37
Principals	05	00	09	08	25	08	02	14	29
Teachers	08	01	16	08	17	06	03	09	31
Parents	04	03	12	13	19	06	03	09	32
TOTAL	07	02	15	10	20	07	03	10	26

TABLE B-6.
Ethnic Distribution of Sample (in percent)

	Negro[1]	Mexican	Oriental	Caucasian
Board Members	00	02	01	97
Superintendents	00	00	00	100
Staff	00	00	00	100
Superintendents/Principals	05	00	00	95
Principals	01	03	01	95
Teachers	01	02	01	96
Parents	04	01	02	93
TOTAL	02	01	01	96

[1] In 1962, the term black had not yet wide currency.

TABLE B-7.

Distribution of (1962) Political Preferences of Sample (in percent)

	Liberal							Conservative	
	(1) Thomas	(2) Bowles	(3) Adlai	(4) JFK	(5) Rocky	(6) Nixon	(7) Goldw	(8) Welch	Average Prefer- ence
Board Member	00	01	09	25	15	28	21	00	5.28
Super- intendents	00	00	19	15	19	44	04	00	4.95
Staff	00	00	11	28	19	32	10	00	5.02
Super- intendents/ Principals	00	00	08	26	29	24	13	00	5.08
Principals	02	03	19	30	12	27	07	00	4.56
Teachers	01	01	13	39	11	24	11	00	4.74
Parents	01	01	10	41	09	25	14	00	4.81

TABLE B-8.   Norms for Intelligence, Defenses, Birth Order, Certainty and Imagination (N = 5847)

Occupation		N	Intelli-gence	Defenses				Birth Order Ord.			Imagina-tion
				Denial	Isola-tion	Projec-tion	Regres-sion	TAS	Position	Certainty	
Board Members		231	39	46	49	42	35	48	26	61	37
Superintendents		57	57	43	46	49	45	44	25	59	46
Staff		232	55	38	47	49	44	46	25	60	48
Superintendents/ Principals		38	47	42	43	44	48	47	31	60	44
Principals		118	50	41	45	46	49	43	26	60	43
Administrators (total)		445	52	41	45	47	47	45	26	60	45
Teachers		3750	43	44	45	49	45	42	24	63	46
Parents		1421	27	45	52	44	43	49	22	62	41
Sex	Male	2573	41	49	48	48	41	40	25	62	46
	Female	3274	36	41	47	47	45	50	23	62	45
Age	Under 35	2105	36	43	46	49	43	42	22	59	50
	36-45	1988	39	45	50	47	45	44	24	61	43
	Over 46	1754	45	41	47	47	44	47	25	66	42
Educa-tion	H. S. diploma		18	49	49	41	45	49	26	65	35
	College degree		32	42	48	45	41	48	23	61	49
	Post-grad.		46	45	46	49	44	43	24	58	46
Politics	Liberal		37	44	49	47	43	44	24	60	47
	Conservative		41	44	47	55	45	45	24	62	43

The most notable results are the following:

1. Superintendents in particular (57) and administrators in general (52) have considerably higher IQ scores than teachers (43), board members (39), and parents (27). Some of these differences, of course, may be because of differences in education.

2. There is a relative lack of correlation of defense preferences with any other variables. Only sex differences seemed significant; men are greater deniers than women, and women more often use turning-against-self. These defense preferences would fit cultural stereotypes. Also political conservatives use projection more often than liberals.

APPENDIX C

SCALING PROCEDURE

All scales, with the exception of COPE, Imagination, and Certainty, were generated in the same way: facet design, dichotomous decisions, Guttman scale.

FACET DESIGN

The facet design is a technique used to describe the total universe of content for a given area of investigation (for example, childhood relations for LIPHE, educational values for VAL-ED). The cells generated by the design are used to construct a series of items aimed at measuring a chosen area. Examples of facet design are given throughout the book. These items are then refined by the method of dichotomous decisions.

DICHOTOMOUS DECISIONS

After a series of items are subjected to a mathematical technique, such as factor analysis or Guttman scaling, aimed at forming them into a scale, there remains the question of whether the resulting items are actually measuring the same content or are simply empirically correlated with each other though differing in content. To test whether items are measuring the same content, Schutz (1950, 1959) introduced the method of dichotomous decisions.

A universe of content is defined and expert judges, usually five, are given a population of items, one to a card. The definitions of the content are presented to the judges as a series of dichotomous decisions. The judges make these decisions successively for each item, until the item comes to rest in a final category. Through the use of a statistic devised for this purpose (Schutz, 1952), the percent of agreement among judges for each dichotomy is computed. An item is said to be an instance of the definition if some predetermined percentage (usually 90 or 95) of judgments agree on the final placement of the item. Figure C.1 shows the dichotomy decision array for FIRO-F.

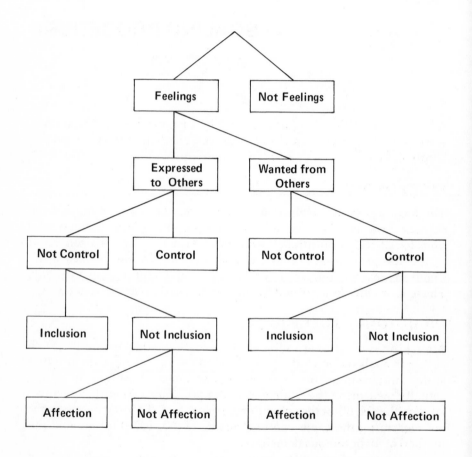

FIGURE C-1.

Dichotomous Decisions for FIRO-F

Each category shown is defined in a sentence or two. Percent agreement is computed for each dichotomy. If judges do not agree on which items belong in which categories, it is a simple matter to discover which dichotomy is unreliable, change the definition of that category and repeat the procedure with new judges. The items with low agreement may be examined and either eliminated or reworded. In this way, the sharpness of the definitions of both items and categories is quickly increased until it is clear that the items do fit the categories. For each scale in this study, this procedure was used to generate twelve items.

These twelve items were administered to a large subgroup of the sample (usually 1000), and the Guttman scaling method was used to reduce these to a nine-item scale.

GUTTMAN SCALING

Of the several techniques for psychological scale construction available, the most appropriate one was the Guttman technique for cumulative scale analysis. For delimited content areas, the Guttman method is more efficient and relevant than other methods such as factor analysis, which are more useful for isolating variables.

The Guttman method has been described at length elsewhere (Guttman, 1950). Scales comprised of items regularly decreasing in popularity are constructed in such a way that any individual will accept items sequentially to a given point and then reject the remainder. If a series of items approximates this cumulative model to the degree that 90 percent of all responses to all items can be predicted correctly from only a knowledge of how many items each person accepted, then the items are said to be *reproducible* and to form a *unidimensional* scale. Unidimensionality means that all items are measuring the same dimension.

For all cumulative scales a length of nine items (ten points) was chosen. This number has the virtues of (1) providing sufficient length for acceptable reliability (stability) of the scale, (2) providing a sufficient number of categories for dividing respondents into as many classes (ten) as are usually needed in psychological research, (3) keeping testing time short, and (4) keeping scoring uniform among scales and in single digits for computational ease.

The twelve items administered to 1000 subjects were given to the GUTS computer program (Schutz & Krasnow, 1964), developed for this project. The aims of the GUTS program are (1) from a set of M-items (in the present case, M = 12), derive the best K-item Guttman scales (K = 9 for this case); (2) assign scale scores to all subjects based on the best of the scales generated; and (3) compute the intensity function (zero point) of each scale (see Guttman, 1950).

The program takes a set of M-items with R response categories (in the present situation, R = 6 in all cases, from *strongly disagree* to *strongly agree*) and dichotomizes each item at every possible cutting point (R = 1 way per item). The program then finds the permutation of items with the highest reproducibility. The three 9-item scales (permutations) with the highest reproducibility are printed out by the computer printer. From these three, the most satisfactory permutation is selected based on the usual criteria for Guttman scaling, including reproducibility, percentage error per item, distribution of scale types, the intensity function, and the consistency of the content of the items.

The reproducibility is computed for every permutation on a test group made up of a randomly selected subset of any size up to S (in this case, S = 1000) of the total population S (in this case, S = 5847). It is then computed for the check group, usually the remainder of the sample. This is to insure that the reproducibility was not due to capitalizing on chance.

Several types of data are provided by the program. The data reported for each scale includes the following:

1. Identification of which nine of the twelve items was selected;
2. The items listed in order by percentage of all subjects accepting the items;
3. The percentage of respondents accepting each item;
4. The cutoff point for dichotomizing the response set for each item;
5. Mean response score on each item for all respondents;
6. Standard deviation for each item;
7. Point of least intensity (zero point);
8. Reproducibility of scale;
9. Percentage of subjects receiving each scale score;
10. Mean scale score;
11. Standard deviation of scale.

APPENDIX D

ADMINISTRATOR EVALUATION SCALES

The original battery of scales, which provided the research foundation for the foregoing book, incorporated all the research scales in this appendix as well as the following scales commercially available from Consulting Psychologists Press, 577 College Avenue, Palo Alto, California 94306: FIRO-F, LIPHE, COPE, VAL-ED. Reproducibility, distribution of scale scores, and other psychometric data are also available from CPP. The battery took respondents two hours to complete. The reproducibility of the original subscales proved extremely high, averaging .929.

The scales in this appendix have been recast as feedback scales. They are best filled out anonymously. The targets are school superintendents and school principals. The respondents are administrative staff members, teachers, and principals of the schools, as well as the school board members and parents of the students. Certain subscales are repeated across scales. For example, the same subscale, Use of Human Resources, is given to the school board, to administrative members, and to principals, in order to evaluate this trait in superintendents.

Within each scale, items have been randomized. The scoring key for each scale, however, is divided into subscales. The subscales are Guttman scales. All subscales are scored in the same manner. Scores range from 0 to 9, with 9 indicating maximum acceptance of the scale name.

When the items in the study were originally used, the words *he* and *him* appeared in references to the principal and the superintendent. In order to eliminate this vestige of sexism, minor changes have been made in the wording of the items. While the instruments were devised for use in selecting and placing public school superintendents and public school principals, their application is far broader. In addition to their use for selection and placement of other high-ranking administrators in public school systems, the two administrator evaluation scales may be useful as feedback instruments in organization development (OD) in schools—to improve interpersonal relations and to identify problems; and as survey instruments—to study school climates. With proper adaptation, the scales may be used for a wide variety of administrator selections and placements outside the educational environment.

Superintendent Feedback Scale—School Board Form

This questionnaire is designed to explore how you perceive the superintendent in this school system. There are, of course, no right or wrong answers. Some items may seem similar to others. However, each item is different, so please answer each one without regard to the others. There is no time limit, but do not debate long over any item.

Directions: For each statement below, decide which of the following answers best applies to you. Place the number of the answer to the left of the statement. Please be honest.

1. Definitely *not* true
2. Not true
3. Tends to be not true

4. Tends to be true
5. True
6. Especially true

_____ 1. It is made clear to me how I can best help the schools.

_____ 2. The superintendent carries out board policies even when opposed to them.

_____ 3. I am allowed the opportunity to participate appropriately in school decisions.

_____ 4. Too many important decisions are made which fail to involve enough people in the process.

_____ 5. I would like the superintendent to feel more strongly that I can be trusted to make wise changes.

_____ 6. I would like the superintendent to feel more strongly that I am important to the district.

_____ 7. I have an important part to play in helping the schools achieve their educational goals.

_____ 8. I would like the superintendent to have more confidence in me as a competent educational leader.

_____ 9. I would like the superintendent to feel more strongly that I am a significant person.

_____10. The superintendent acts as though he has little faith in the board's ability to deal with instructional problems.

_____11. Efforts are made to hire the best people available for each position.

_____12. I would like the superintendent to feel more convivial with me.

_____13. Recognition is given whenever I make an important contribution to school policy and program.

_____14. I would like the superintendent to be more interested in my performance.

Superintendent Feedback Scale—School Board Form

_____15. I would like the superintendent to feel more at ease with me.

_____16. I would like the superintendent to believe more strongly that my function is a significant one.

_____17. I would like the superintendent to have more respect for my ability to select personnel.

_____18. I would like the superintendent to feel more strongly that I am a competent decision-maker.

_____19. I would like the superintendent to have more respect for my ability to think critically.

_____20. I would like the superintendent to have more respect for my judgment.

_____21. I would like the superintendent to be more concerned with my ideas.

_____22. The needs and desires of the staff are *not* perceived.

_____23. I would like the superintendent to have more respect for my administrative abilities.

_____24. The superintendent readily makes available to the board information that it requests.

_____25. I would like the superintendent to feel more interest in my development as a person.

_____26. I would like the superintendent to be more confident that I am a self-sufficient person.

_____27. The superintendent will not defend his or her beliefs and ideas if the board seems to disagree with them.

_____28. I would like the superintendent to feel more like a pal toward me.

_____29. The superintendent is willing to defend a position on issues that he or she feels are right.

_____30. I would like the superintendent to have more admiration for my ability to be creative.

_____31. Routine use is made of the best informed people on the staff for solving problems.

_____32. I would like the superintendent to feel more informal with me.

_____33. I would like the superintendent to be more cordial toward me.

_____34. The superintendent keeps the board informed of possible problems so that they can act in time.

Superintendent Feedback Scale—School Board Form

_____35. I would like the superintendent to be more involved in my efforts to succeed.

_____36. People who will be affected by a decision are involved in the process of reaching it.

_____37. I would like the superintendent to feel more relaxed with me.

_____38. I would like the superintendent to feel more like joking with me once in a while.

_____39. Wise use is made of people who do things well.

_____40. Staff members know the reasons underlying decisions.

_____41. The superintendent is overly aggressive in approaching board members.

_____42. I would like the superintendent to feel more strongly that I am part of a significant educational body.

_____43. The superintendent is cooperative in his dealings with the board.

_____44. I try to inform myself about recent developments in education and take other actions which will help me do my job more effectively.

_____45. I am kept informed as to how I am doing at frequent intervals so that I know what needs improvement.

_____46. I would like the superintendent to feel more like a friend toward me.

_____47. The superintendent gives recognition for the time and effort I expend.

_____48. Things are well planned so that they are accomplished on time.

_____49. I am kept informed as to how I may participate in making school policy and programs.

_____50. Opportunity is provided for me to contribute extra time to the schools.

_____51. It is made clear to groups or persons asked to make recommendations whether their work will become policy or simply be considered as advice.

_____52. I would like the superintendent to like me more.

_____53. The superintendent suggests reasonable policies for the consideration of the board.

_____54. I would like the superintendent to feel more strongly that I am an interesting person.

SCORING THE SUPERINTENDENT FEEDBACK SCALE
SCHOOL BOARD FORM

Instructions: Using this form as a worksheet, you will derive six scores. For example, the answer key to Use of Human Resources—School Board is in the first column below. Compare the actual response to each item with the keyed responses. If the response matches one of the numbers in the key, place a check mark in front of the item number of this worksheet. Count the number of checks and enter that score in the box below the key. Score the remaining scales in the same manner.

SCALE NAME:	I am well motivated, guided, and given an opportunity to do my best for the schools.		The superintendent deals effectively with the school board.		I would like the superintendent to feel friendlier toward me.	
SHORT TITLE:	USE OF HUMAN RESOURCES		BOARD RELATIONS		LIKING	
	Item	Key	Item	Key	Item	Key
	1)	6	2)	6	12)	3-4-5-6
	3)	5-6	10)	1-2	15)	4-5-6
	7)	6	24)	6	28)	3-4-5-6
	13)	5-6	27)	1-2	32)	3-4-5-6
	44)	5-6	29)	6	33)	3-4-5-6
	45)	5-6	34)	5-6	37)	3-4-5-6
	47)	5-6	41)	1-2	38)	2-3-4-5-6
	49)	5-6	43)	6	46)	4-5-6
	50)	6	53)	6	52)	3-4-5-6
	UHR ☐		BR ☐		LIK ☐	

SCALE NAME:	I would like the superintendent to feel more strongly that I am an interesting person in a significant role.		I would like the superintendent to have more respect and confidence in my abilities.		The administrator organizes activities so as to obtain maximum benefit from district resources.	
SHORT TITLE:	IMPORTANCE		COMPETENCE		ORGANIZATION	
	Item	Key	Item	Key	Item	Key
	6)	3-4-5-6	5)	4-5-6	4)	1-2
	9)	4-5-6	8)	3-4-5-6	11)	6
	14)	4-5-6	17)	3-4-5-6	22)	1-2-3
	16)	4-5-6	18)	3-4-5-6	31)	6
	21)	3-4-5-6	19)	4-5-6	36)	5-6
	25)	4-5-6	20)	3-4-5-6	39)	5-6
	35)	3-4-5-6	23)	4-5-6	40)	5-6
	42)	3-4-5-6	26)	3-4-5-6	48)	5-6
	54)	3-4-5-6	30)	3-4-5-6	51)	5-6
	IMP ☐		COMP ☐		ORG ☐	

Superintendent Feedback Scale— Administrative Staff Form

This questionnaire is designed to explore how you perceive the superintendent in this school system. There are, of course, no right or wrong answers. Some items may seem similar to others. However, each item is different so please answer each one without regard to the others. There is no time limit, but do not debate long over any item.

Directions: For each statement below, decide which of the following answers best applies to you. Place the number of the answer on the line at the left of the statement. Please be honest.

1. Definitely *not* true
2. Not true
3. Tends to be not true

4. Tends to be true
5. True
6. Especially true

_____ 1. I am allowed the opportunity to participate appropriately in school educations.

_____ 2. I would like the superintendent to feel more like a friend toward me.

_____ 3. I would like the superintendent to feel more strongly that I am a significant person.

_____ 4. Solutions, once agreed upon, reflect critical and logical thinking.

_____ 5. I would like the superintendent to feel more interest in my development as a person.

_____ 6. The superintendent carries out board policies even when opposed to them.

_____ 7. I would like the superintendent to have more admiration for my ability to be creative.

_____ 8. I would like the superintendent to feel more strongly that I can be trusted to make wise changes.

_____ 9. The superintendent is willing to defend a position on issues that he or she feels are right.

_____10. Unique possible solutions are considered for school problems.

_____11. The superintendent has little faith in the board's ability to deal with instructional problems.

_____12. Sources of information are weighed carefully.

_____13. I am kept informed as to how I may participate in making school policy and programs.

_____14. I would like the superintendent to be more cordial toward me.

Superintendent Feedback Scale— Administrative Staff Form

_____15. Situations in the school where real problems exist are recognized and acknowledged.

_____16. The superintendent is cooperative in his dealings with the board.

_____17. Possible solutions to a problem are weighed carefully.

_____18. I would like the superintendent to feel more informal with me.

_____19. Opportunity is provided for me to contribute extra time to the schools.

_____20. I would like the superintendent to be more interested in my performance.

_____21. I try to inform myself about recent developments in education and take other actions which will help me do my job more effectively.

_____22. I would like the superintendent to feel more relaxed with me.

_____23. I would like the superintendent to feel more like a pal toward me.

_____24. I would like the superintendent to have more confidence in me as a competent educational leader.

_____25. The superintendent is overly aggressive in approaching board members.

_____26. I would like the superintendent to feel more convivial with me.

_____27. The superintendent keeps the board informed of possible problems so that they can act in time.

_____28. I would like the superintendent to have more respect for my ability to select personnel.

_____29. I would like the superintendent to believe more strongly that my function is a significant one.

_____30. Recognition is given whenever I make an important contribution to school policy and program.

_____31. I would like the superintendent to be more confident that I am a self-sufficient person.

_____32. I would like the superintendent to feel more like joking with me once in a while.

_____33. The superintendent will not defend beliefs and ideas that the board seems to disagree with.

_____34. I would like the superintendent to have more respect for my judgment.

Superintendent Feedback Scale— Administrative Staff Form

_____35. I would like the superintendent to be more concerned with my ideas.

_____36. I would like the superintendent to have more respect for my administrative abilities.

_____37. I would like the superintendent to feel more strongly that I am part of a significant educational body.

_____38. All the elements relating to problems or issues are taken into account.

_____39. The superintendent gives recognition for the time and effort I expend.

_____40. I would like the superintendent to feel more at ease with me.

_____41. All relevant information is obtained before decisions are made.

_____42. I would like the superintendent to feel more strongly that I am a competent decision-maker.

_____43. I have an important part to play in helping the schools achieve their educational goals.

_____44. I would like the superintendent to like me more.

_____45. The superintendent suggests reasonable policies for the consideration of the board.

_____46. I would like the superintendent to have more respect for my ability to think critically.

_____47. I would like the superintendent to be more involved in my efforts to succeed.

_____48. I am kept informed as to how I am doing at frequent intervals so that I know what needs improvement.

_____49. It is made clear to me how I can best help the schools.

_____50. Consideration is given to the important implications of a course of action.

_____51. I would like the superintendent to feel more strongly that I am an interesting person.

_____52. The superintendent readily makes available to the board information that it requests.

_____53. Possible problems or issues are anticipated.

_____54. I would like the superintendent to feel more strongly that I am important to the district.

SCORING THE SUPERINTENDENT FEEDBACK SCALE
ADMINISTRATIVE STAFF FORM

Instructions: Using this form as a worksheet, you will derive six scores. For example, the answer key to Use of Human Resources – Administrative Staff is in the first column below. Compare the actual response to each item with the keyed responses. If the response matches one of the numbers in the key, place a check mark in front of the item number of this worksheet. Count the number of checks and enter that score in the box below the key. Score the remaining scales in the same manner.

SCALE NAME:	I am well motivated, guided, and given an opportunity to do my best for the schools.	The superintendent deals effectively with the school board.	The administrator facilitates efficient solution of school problems.
SHORT TITLE:	**USE OF HUMAN RESOURCES**	**BOARD RELATIONS**	**DECISION MAKING**

Item	Key	Item	Key	Item	Key
1)	5-6	6)	6	4)	5-6
13)	5-6	9)	6	10)	4-5-6
19)	6	11)	1-2	12)	5-6
21)	5-6	16)	6	15)	5-6
30)	5-6	25)	1-2	17)	4-5-6
39)	5-6	27)	5-6	38)	5-6
43)	6	33)	1-2	41)	5-6
48)	5-6	45)	6	50)	5-6
49)	6	52)	6	53)	6

UHR ☐   BR ☐   DM ☐

SCALE NAME:	I would like the superintendent to feel more strongly that I am an interesting person in a significant role.	I would like the superintendent to have more respect and confidence in my abilities.	I would like the superintendent to feel friendlier toward me.
SHORT TITLE:	**IMPORTANCE**	**COMPETENCE**	**LIKING**

Item	Key	Item	Key	Item	Key
3)	4-5-6	7)	3-4-5-6	2)	4-5-6
5)	4-5-6	8)	4-5-6	14)	3-4-5-6
20)	4-5-6	24)	3-4-5-6	18)	3-4-5-6
29)	4-5-6	28)	3-4-5-6	22)	3-4-5-6
35)	3-4-5-6	31)	3-4-5-6	23)	3-4-5-6
37)	3-4-5-6	34)	3-4-5-6	26)	3-4-5-6
47)	3-4-5-6	36)	4-5-6	32)	2-3-4-5-6
51)	3-4-5-6	42)	3-4-5-6	40)	4-5-6
54)	3-4-5-6	46)	4-5-6	44)	3-4-5-6

IMP ☐   COMP ☐   LIK ☐

Superintendent Feedback Scale—Principal Form

This questionnaire is designed to explore how you perceive the superintendent in this school system. There are, of course, no right or wrong answers. Some items may seem similar to others. However, each item is different so please answer each one without regard to the others. There is no time limit, but do not debate long over any item.

Directions: For each statement below, decide which of the following answers best applies to you. Place the number of the answer on the line at the left of the statement. Please be honest.

1. Definitely *not* true
2. Not true
3. Tends to be not true

4. Tends to be true
5. True
6. Especially true

_____ 1. The superintendent will not defend beliefs and ideas that the board seems to disagree with.

_____ 2. I am kept informed as to how I may participate in making school policy and programs.

_____ 3. Things are well planned so that they are accomplished on time.

_____ 4. It is made clear to groups or persons asked to make recommendations whether their work will become policy or simply be considered as advice.

_____ 5. Efforts are made to hire the best people available for each position.

_____ 6. The superintendent keeps the board informed of possible problems so that they can act in time.

_____ 7. Routine use is made of the best informed people on the staff for solving problems.

_____ 8. Opportunity is provided for me to contribute extra time to the schools.

_____ 9. At frequent intervals, I am kept informed as to how I am doing so that I know what needs improvement.

_____10. Recognition is given whenever I make an important contribution to school policy and program.

_____11. Wise use is made of people who do things well.

_____12. I am allowed the opportunity to participate appropriately in school decisions.

Superintendent Feedback Scale—Principal Form

_____13. People who will be affected by a decision are involved in the process of reaching it.

_____14. The superintendent acts as though he has little faith in the board's ability to deal with instructional problems.

_____15. The superintendent is willing to defend a position on issues that he or she feels is right.

_____16. Staff members know the reasons underlying decisions.

_____17. I try to inform myself about recent developments in education and take other actions which will help me do my job more effectively.

_____18. The superintendent readily makes available to the board information that it requests.

_____19. The needs and desires of the staff are *not* perceived.

_____20. The superintendent is cooperative in his dealings with the board.

_____21. The superintendent suggests reasonable policies even when opposed to them.

_____22. Too many important decisions are made which fail to involve enough people in the process.

_____23. The superintendent is overly aggressive in approaching board members.

_____24. The superintendent carries out board policies even when opposed to them.

_____25. The superintendent gives recognition for the time and effort I expend.

_____26. It is made clear to me how I can best help the schools.

_____27. I have an important part to play in helping the schools achieve their educational goals.

SCORING THE SUPERINTENDENT FEEDBACK SCALE
PRINCIPAL FORM

Instructions: Using this form as a worksheet, you will derive three scores. For example, the answer key to Use of Human Resources—Principals is in the first column below. Compare the actual response to each item with the keyed responses. If the response matches one of the numbers in the key, place a check mark in front of the item number of this worksheet. Count the number of checks and enter that score in the box below the key. Score the remaining scales in the same manner.

SCALE NAME:	I am well motivated, guided, and given an opportunity to do my best for the schools.	The superintendent deals effectively with the school board.	The administrator organizes activities so as to obtain maximum benefit from district resources.
SHORT TITLE:	**USE OF HUMAN RESOURCES**	**BOARD RELATIONS**	**ORGANIZATION**

Item	Key	Item	Key	Item	Key
2)	5-6	1)	1-2	3)	1-2-3
8)	6	6)	5-6	4)	5-6
9)	5-6	14)	1-2	5)	6
10)	5-6	15)	6	7)	6
12)	5-6	18)	6	11)	5-6
17)	5-6	20)	6	13)	5-6
27)	6	21)	6	16)	5-6
25)	5-6	23)	1-2	19)	1-2-3
26)	6	24)	6	22)	1-2

UHR ☐   BR ☐   ORG ☐

School Feedback Scale—Community Form

This questionnaire is designed to explore how you perceive this school system. There are, of course, no right or wrong answers. Some items may seem similar to others. However, each item is different so please answer each one without regard to the others. There is no time limit, but do not debate long over any item.

Directions: For each statement below, decide which of the following answers best applies to you. Place the number of the answer on the line at the left of the statement. Please be honest.

1. Definitely *not* true
2. Not true
3. Tends to be not true

4. Tends to be true
5. True
6. Especially true

_____ 1. Solutions, once agreed upon, reflect critical and logical thinking.

_____ 2. I am kept informed as to how I may participate in making school policy and programs.

_____ 3. The school is doing the best possible job of educating students.

_____ 4. Possible problems or issues are anticipated.

_____ 5. I really like the school and take pride in it.

_____ 6. The principal gives recognition for the time and effort I spend.

_____ 7. The schools give recognition whenever I make an important contribution to school policy and program.

_____ 8. I really believe that I have an important part to play in helping the school achieve its educational goals.

_____ 9. Opportunity is provided for me to contribute time to the school.

_____10. School personnel act very friendly and personal towards me.

_____11. Possible solutions to a problem are weighed carefully.

_____12. The schools allow me the opportunity to participate appropriately in school policy decisions.

_____13. All the elements relating to problems or issues are taken into account.

_____14. Unique possible solutions are considered for school problems.

_____15. All relevant information is obtained before decisions are made.

School Feedback Scale—Community Form

_____16. Consideration is given to the important implications of a course of action.

_____17. Situations in the school where real problems exist are recognized and acknowledged.

_____18. Sources of information are weighed carefully.

SCORING THE SCHOOL FEEDBACK SCALE
COMMUNITY FORM

Instructions: Using this form as a worksheet, you will derive two scores. For example, the answer key to Use of Human Resources—Community is in the first column below. Compare the actual response to each item with the keyed responses. If the response matches one of the numbers in the key, place a check mark in front of the item number of this worksheet. Count the number of checks and enter that score in the box below the key. Score the Decision-Making scale in the same manner.

SCALE NAME:	I am well motivated, pre-pared, and given an oppor-tunity to do my best for the schools.	The administrator facilitates efficient solution of school problems.
SHORT TITLE:	USE OF HUMAN RESOURCES	DECISION MAKING

Item	Key	Item	Key
2)	5-6	1)	5-6
3)	6	4)	6
5)	5-6	11)	4-5-6
6)	5-6	13)	5-6
7)	5-6	14)	4-5-6
8)	5-6	15)	5-6
9)	4-5-6	16)	5-6
10)	5-6	17)	5-6
12)	5-6	18)	5-6

UHR ☐   DM ☐

Principal Feedback Scale— Administrative Staff Form

This questionnaire is designed to explore how you perceive the principal in this school. There are, of course, no right or wrong answers. Some items may seem similar to others. However, each item is different so please answer each one without regard to the others. There is no time limit, but do not debate long over any item.

Directions: For each statement below, decide which of the following answers best applies to you. Place the number of the answer on the line at the left of the statement. Please be honest.

1. Definitely *not* true
2. Not true
3. Tends to be not true

4. Tends to be true
5. True
6. Especially true

_____ 1. I would like the principal to like me more.

_____ 2. I would like the principal to feel more strongly that my function is a significant one.

_____ 3. I would like the principal to have more respect for my intellectual abilities.

_____ 4. I would like the principal to feel more like joking with me once in a while.

_____ 5. I would like the principal to feel more like a pal to me.

_____ 6. I would like the principal to have more confidence in me as a competent instructor.

_____ 7. I would like the principal to believe more strongly in my worth as a professional person.

_____ 8. I would like the principal to feel closer to me as a person.

_____ 9. I would like the principal to have more respect for my ability to think critically.

_____10. I would like the principal to feel more cordiality toward me.

_____11. I would like the principal to feel more strongly that I am a competent instructor.

_____12. I would like the principal to feel more strongly that I am an interesting person.

_____13. I would like the principal to feel more strongly that I am important.

_____14. I would like the principal to feel more at ease with me.

Principal Feedback Scale— Administrative Staff Form

_____15. I would like the principal to feel more strongly that I am important for the school.

_____16. I would like the principal to have more admiration for my ability to be creative.

_____17. I would like the principal to feel more informal with me.

_____18. I would like the principal to feel more strongly that I can make competent decisions.

_____19. I would like the principal to have more respect for my judgment.

_____20. I would like the principal to feel more strongly that my role is a significant one.

_____21. I would like the principal to feel friendlier toward me.

_____22. I would like the principal to be more concerned with my ideas.

_____23. I would like the principal to be more concerned with me as a person.

_____24. I would like the principal to feel more strongly that I can be trusted to suggest wise changes.

_____25. I would like the principal to feel more strongly that I am self-sufficient as a person.

_____26. I would like the principal to be more interested in my performance.

_____27. I would like the principal to feel more convivial with me.

SCORING THE PRINCIPAL FEEDBACK SCALE
ADMINISTRATIVE STAFF FORM

Instructions: Using this form as a worksheet, you will derive three scores. For example, the answer key to Importance is in the first column below. Compare the actual response to each item with the keyed responses. If the response matches one of the numbers in the key, place a check mark in front of the item number of this worksheet. Count the number of checks and enter that score in the box below the key. Score the remaining scales in the same manner.

SCALE NAME:	I would like the principal to feel more strongly that I am an interesting person in an important position.	I would like the principal to have more respect and confidence in my abilities.	I would like the principal to feel friendlier toward me and to like me more.
SHORT TITLE:	**IMPORTANCE**	**COMPETENCE**	**LIKING**

Item	Key	Item	Key	Item	Key
2)	4-5-6	3)	5-6	1)	4-5-6
7)	5-6	6)	3-4-5-6	4)	3-4-5-6
12)	4-5-6	9)	4-5-6	5)	3-4-5-6
13)	3-4-5-6	11)	4-5-6	8)	3-4-5-6
15)	3-4-5-6	16)	3-4-5-6	10)	3-4-5-6
20)	4-5-6	18)	5-6	14)	4-5-6
22)	3-4-5-6	19)	4-5-6	17)	4-5-6
23)	3-4-5-6	24)	3-4-5-6	21)	3-4-5-6
26)	5-6	25)	4-5-6	27)	3-4-5-6

IMP ☐	COMP ☐	LIK ☐

Principal Feedback Scale—Teacher Form

This questionnaire is designed to explore how you perceive the principal in this school. There are, of course, no right or wrong answers. Some items may seem similar to others. However, each item is different so please answer each one without regard to the others. There is no time limit, but do not debate long over any item.

Directions: For each statement below, decide which of the following answers best applies to you. Place the number of the answer on the line at the left of the statement. Please be honest.

1. Definitely *not* true
2. Not true
3. Tends to be not true

4. Tends to be true
5. True
6. Especially true

_____ 1. There is an adequate system for reporting the progress of pupils to their parents.

_____ 2. New ideas and information relating to education are regularly discussed.

_____ 3. I would like the principal to like me more.

_____ 4. Teachers are kept informed as to how their work is evaluated.

_____ 5. I would like the principal to believe more strongly in my worth as a professional person.

_____ 6. Teachers are not overloaded with non-teaching assignments, such as hall duty, yard supervision.

_____ 7. I would like the principal to feel more informal with me.

_____ 8. I would like the principal to feel closer to me as a person.

_____ 9. I would like the principal to have more respect for my ability to think critically.

_____10. Recognition is given for the time and effort I expend.

_____11. All relevant information is obtained before decisions are made.

_____12. I would like the principal to feel more cordiality toward me.

_____13. I would like the principal to feel more strongly that my function is a significant one.

_____14. An effective system of pupil discipline is supported and maintained.

_____15. I would like the principal to have more respect for my judgment.

_____16. High standards of academic achievement and learning are expected of the students.

Principal Feedback Scale—Teacher Form

_____17. Experimentation and new approaches in instruction occur reasonably often.

_____18. I would like the principal to feel more like joking with me once in a while.

_____19. An effective system of guidance for the pupils is supported and maintained.

_____20. The staff has a good knowledge of the feelings and opinions of the children about the school.

_____21. Staff members know how people feel about the school and about its program.

_____22. The staff's attention is called to important and interesting articles or publications.

_____23. I would like the principal to be more concerned with me as a person.

_____24. Recognition is given whenever I make an important contribution to school policy and program.

_____25. I would like the principal to feel more strongly that I am an interesting person.

_____26. I would like the principal to be more interested in my performance.

_____27. I would like the principal to feel more strongly that I am a competent instructor.

_____28. I would like the principal to have more admiration for my ability to be creative.

_____29. All the elements relating to problems or issues are taken into account.

_____30. Solutions, once agreed upon reflect critical and logical thinking.

_____31. Situations in the school where real problems exist are recognized and acknowledged.

_____32. I would like the principal to have more confidence in me as a competent instructor.

_____33. Released time is available for teachers to work on special projects or ideas designed to improve the school program.

_____34. Adequate help and supervision are provided for teachers.

_____35. I would like the principal to feel more strongly that I am self-sufficient as a person.

_____36. I would like the principal to feel friendlier toward me.

Principal Feedback Scale—Teacher Form

_____37. I would like the principal to feel more strongly that I am important for the school.

_____38. Teachers are kept informed of central office policy changes affecting the school.

_____39. I would like the principal to feel more strongly that I can make competent decisions.

_____40. Information is regularly available on such things as new teaching materials, new aids, and new resources.

_____41. Teachers and parents feel free to make suggestions for improving the school.

_____42. Possible solutions to a problem are weighed carefully.

_____43. Buildings and grounds are maintained in a satisfactory and attractive manner.

_____44. Opportunity is provided for me to contribute extra time to the school.

_____45. I am kept informed as to how I may participate in making school policy and programs.

_____46. I would like the principal to feel more strongly that I am important.

_____47. Schedules required for the effective operation of the school are made.

_____48. The community and parents are kept aware of the accomplishments of the school and the students.

_____49. I would like the principal to feel more strongly that my role is a significant one.

_____50. Unique possible solutions are considered for school problems.

_____51. Staff members discuss their problems and concerns freely with each other.

_____52. At frequent intervals, I am kept informed as to how I am doing so that I know what needs improvement.

_____53. Adequate materials needed for instruction are available.

_____54. I would like the principal to be more concerned with my ideas.

_____55. The principal helps me to do the best possible job of educating students.

_____56. There is constant evaluation of the total learning process.

Principal Feedback Scale—Teacher Form

_____57. The principal makes clear to me how I can best help the school.

_____58. Current events of significance and importance for the school are regularly discussed.

_____59. New developments in each subject area are called to the staff's attention.

_____60. I would like the principal to feel more strongly that I can be trusted to suggest wise changes.

_____61. Extra-curricular activities are organized so that they function smoothly.

_____62. There is good communication between the teachers and other members of the school staff.

_____63. I would like the principal to feel more convivial with me.

_____64. I really like the school and take pride in it.

_____65. I am allowed the opportunity to participate appropriately in school policy decisions.

_____66. Sources of information are weighed carefully.

_____67. Possible problems or issues are anticipated.

_____68. I would like the principal to have more respect for my intellectual abilities.

_____69. I would like the principal to feel more like a pal with me.

_____70. I would like the principal to feel more at ease with me.

_____71. Consideration is given to the important implications of a course of action.

_____72. Teachers express their opinions and feelings freely.

SCORING THE PRINCIPAL FEEDBACK SCALE
TEACHER FORM

Instructions: Using this form as a worksheet, you will derive eight scores. For example, the answer key to Decision Making is in the first column below. Compare the actual response to each item with the keyed responses. If the response matches one of the numbers in the key, place a check mark in front of the item number of this worksheet. Count the number of checks and enter that score in the box below the key. Score the remaining scales in the same manner.

SCALE NAME:

Scale	Description
DECISION MAKING	The administrator facilitates efficient solution of school problems.
USE OF HUMAN RESOURCES	I am well motivated, prepared, and given an opportunity to do my best for the schools.
SCHOOL MAINTENANCE	Matters such as schedules, assignments, building maintenance, availability of teaching materials, and establishing systems for doing the work of the school are well taken care of.
COMMUNICATION	The principal maintains an effective system of communication.

SHORT TITLE:

DECISION MAKING

Item	Key
1)	5-6
29)	5-6
30)	5-6
31)	5-6
42)	4-5-6
50)	4-5-6
66)	5-6
67)	6
71)	5-6

DM [ ]

USE OF HUMAN RESOURCES

Item	Key
10)	4-5-6
24)	3-4-5-6
44)	4-5-6
45)	5-6
52)	4-5-6
55)	5-6
57)	6
64)	5-6
65)	5-6

UHR [ ]

SCHOOL MAINTENANCE

Item	Key
1)	3-4-5-6
6)	3-4-5-6
14)	3-4-5-6
19)	3-4-5-6
34)	3-4-5-6
43)	3-4-5-6
47)	3-4-5-6
53)	3-4-5-6
61)	3-4-5-6

SM [ ]

COMMUNICATION

Item	Key
4)	4-5-6
20)	5-6
21)	4-5-6
38)	6
41)	5-6
48)	5-6
51)	4-5-6
62)	4-5-6
72)	3-4-5-6

COM [ ]

SCORING THE PRINCIPAL FEEDBACK SCALE
TEACHER FORM (CONTINUED)

SCALE NAME:

SHORT TITLE:

I would like the principal to have more respect and confidence in my abilities.		The principal provides a high level of educational leadership.		I would like the principal to feel strongly that I am an interesting person in an important position.		I would like the principal to feel friendlier toward me and to like me more.	
COMPETENCE		**LEADERSHIP**		**IMPORTANCE**		**LIKING**	
Item	Key	Item	Key	Item	Key	Item	Key
9)	4-5-6	2)	4-5-6	5)	5-6	3)	4-5-6
15)	4-5-6	16)	5-6	13)	4-5-6	7)	4-5-6
27)	4-5-6	17)	4-5-6	23)	3-4-5-6	8)	3-4-5-6
28)	3-4-5-6	22)	4-5-6	25)	4-5-6	12)	3-4-5-6
32)	3-4-5-6	33)	5-6	26)	5-6	18)	3-4-5-6
35)	4-5-6	40)	5-6	37)	3-4-5-6	36)	3-4-5-6
39)	5-6	56)	3-4-5-6	46)	3-4-5-6	63)	3-4-5-6
60)	3-4-5-6	58)	5-6	49)	4-5-6	69)	3-4-5-6
68)	5-6	59)	5-6	54)	3-4-5-6	70)	4-5-6

COMP [ ]   LEAD [ ]   IMP [ ]   LIK [ ]

references

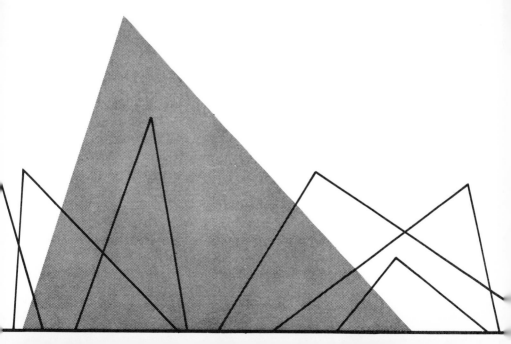

REFERENCES

Adorno, T., Frenkel-Brunswik, E., Levinson, D., & Sanford, R. *The authoritarian personality.* New York: Harper & Row, 1950.

Aichhorn, A. *Wayward youth.* New York: Viking, 1935.

Alexander, F. *Fundamentals of psychoanalysis.* New York: Norton, 1948.

Alexander, F., & Ross, H. *Dynamic psychiatry.* Chicago: University of Chicago Press, 1952.

Allport, G. W. *Personality and social encounter.* Boston: Beacon Press, 1960.

Allport, G. W. *Pattern and growth in personality.* New York: Holt, Rinehart and Winston, 1961.

Anderson, V., & Davies, D. R. *Patterns of educational leadership.* Englewood Cliffs, N.J.: Prentice-Hall, 1956.

Anderson, W., Bauchamp, M., & Cope, W. *The responsibilities of school administrators.* Dept. of Administration and Supervision, New York University, 1952. Mimeographed.

Argyris, C. *Personality and organization: The conflict between system and organization.* New York: Harper & Row, 1957.

Argyris, C. Organization leadership. In L. Petrullo & B. M. Bass (Eds.), *Leadership and interpersonal behavior.* New York: Holt, Rinehart and Winston, 1961.

Argyris, C. *Interpersonal competence and organizational effectiveness.* London: Tavistock Publications, 1962.

Bandura, A., Ross, D., & Ross, S. Vicarious reinforcement and imitative learning. *Journal of Abnormal Social Psychology,* 1963, 67, 601-607.

Barber, B. *Social stratification: A comparative analysis of structure and process.* New York: Harcourt Brace Jovanovich, 1957.

Barnard, C. I. *The functions of the executive.* Cambridge, Mass.: Harvard University Press, 1938.

Barr, A. S., *et al. Wisconsin studies of the measurement and prediction of teacher effectiveness*. Madison, Wis.: Dembar Publications, 1961.

Bass, B. M. Some observations about a general theory of leadership and interpersonal behavior. In L. Petrullo & B. M. Bass (Eds.), *Leadership and interpersonal behavior*. New York: Holt, Rinehart and Winston, 1961.

Bavelas, A. Group size, interaction and structural environment. In B. Schaffner (Ed.), *Group processes: Transactions of the fourth conference, 1957*. New York: Josiah Macy, Jr. Foundation, 1959.

Bennis, W. G. Leadership theory and administrative behavior. In W. G. Bennis, K. D. Benne, & R. Chin (Eds.), *The planning of change*. New York: Holt, Rinehart and Winston, 1961.

Blake, R. R., Mouton, J. S., & Bidwell, A. C. Managerial grid. *Advanced Management Office Executive*, 1962, *1*, 12-15.

Blau, P. M., Gustad, J. W., Jessor, R., Parnes, H. S., & Wilcock, R. C. Occupational choice: A conceptual framework. *Industrial Labor Relations Review*, 1956, *9*, 531-543.

Borg, W. R., Burr, V. F., & Sylvester, A. *Four criteria of principal effectiveness*. Logan, Utah: Utah State University, 1961.

Britton, E. R. Leadership in defining goals for schools. *Educational Leadership*, 1959, *17*, 16-20.

Bronfenbrenner, U. Some familial antecedents of responsibility and leadership in adolescents. In L. Petrullo & B. M. Bass (Eds.), *Leadership and interpersonal behavior*. New York: Holt, Rinehart and Winston, 1961.

Bronowski, J. The values of science. In A. H. Maslow (Ed.), *New knowledge in human values*. New York: Harper & Row, 1959.

Bronson, W. C., Katten, E. S., & Livson, N. Patterns of authority and affection in two generations. *Journal of Abnormal Social Psychology*, 1959, *58*, 143-152.

Bullock, R. P. *School-community attitude analysis for educational administrators*. Columbus, Ohio: College of Education, Ohio State University, 1959.

California school directory, 1961-1962. Burlingame, Calif.: California Association of Secondary School Administrators, 1962.

Campbell, R. F., & Gregg, R. T. (Eds.). *Administrative behavior in education*. New York: Harper & Row, 1957.

Campbell, R. F., & Lipham, J. M. (Eds.). *Administrative theory as a guide to action*. Chicago: Chicago Midwest Administration Center, University of Chicago, 1960.

Capra, P. C., & Dittes, J. E. Birth order as a selective factor among volunteer subjects. *Journal of Abnormal Social Psychology*, 1962, *64*, 302.

Carnap, R. *Logical foundations of probability*. Chicago: University of Chicago Press, 1950.

Carter, R. F. *Communities and their schools* (Technical report). School of Education, Stanford University, 1960.

Chernoff, H., & Moses, L. E. *Elementary decision theory*. New York: John Wiley, 1959.

Christiansen, B. *Attitudes toward foreign affairs as a function of personality.* Oslo: Oslo University Press, 1959.

Cohen, A. Experimental effects of ego-defense preference on interpersonal relations. *Journal of Abnormal Social Psychology*, 1956, *52*, 19-27.

Coladarci, A. P. The administrative-success criteria. *Phi Delta Kappan*, 1955, *37*, 283-285.

Coleman, S. S. *The adolescent society*. Glencoe, Ill.: Free Press, 1961.

Cook, L., & Cook, E. *School problems in human relations*. New York: McGraw-Hill, 1957.

Counts, G. S. *Decision-making and American values in administration*. New York: Teachers College, Columbia University, 1954.

Cox, F. N. An assessment of children's attitudes towards parent figures. *Child Development*, 1962, *33*, 821-830.

Criswell, J. H. The sociometric study of leadership. In L. Petrullo & B. M. Bass (Eds.), *Leadership and interpersonal behavior*. New York: Holt, Rinehart and Winston, 1961.

Culbertson, J. A. (Ed.). *Administrative relationships*. Englewood Cliffs, N.J.: Prentice-Hall, 1960.

Curti, M. *The social ideas of American educators*. Patterson, N.J.: Pageant Books, 1959.

Dahlke, H. O. Value tangle and educational malaise. *The National Elementary Principal*, 1962, *42*, 18-23.

Davis, A. *Social-class influences upon learning*. Cambridge, Mass.: Harvard University Press, 1948.

Delwood, D. Can superintendents perceive community viewpoints? *Administrator's Notebook*. Chicago: Midwest Administration Center, University of Chicago. November, 1959.

Dewey, J. *Democracy and education*. New York: Macmillan, 1922.

Dooher, M. J. (Ed.). *Selection of management personnel*. New York: American Management Association, 1957.

Dubin, R. *Human relations in administration* (2nd ed.). New York: Prentice-Hall, 1961.

Ebel, R. L. Procedures for the analysis of classroom tests. *Educational and Psychological Measurement*, 1954, *14*, 352-364.

Edwards, A. *Population: Comparative occupational statistics for the United States, 1870-1940*. Washington, D.C.: Bureau of the Census, U.S. Department of Commerce, 1943.

208   Leaders of Schools

Elder, G. H. Parental power legitimation and its effect on the adolescent. *Sociometry*, 1963, *26*, 50-65.

Etzioni, A. *A comparative analysis of complex organizations: On power, involvement, and their correlates*. Glencoe, Ill.: Free Press, 1961.

Everett, S. Values in curriculum decision-making. *Association for Supervision and Curriculum Development Yearbook*, 1961, 33-48.

Fenichel, C. *The psychoanalytic theory of neurosis*. New York: Norton, 1945.

Fiedler, F. E. *Leader attitudes and group effectiveness: Final report of ONR project NR170-106, N6-ori-07135*. Urbana, Ill.: University of Illinois Press, 1958.

Fisher, R. A., & Yates, F. *Statistical tables for biological, agricultural, and medical research*. Edinburgh: Oliver and Boyd, 1938. (Reprinted in Table 18 of E. F. Lindquist, *Statistical analysis in educational research*. Boston: Houghton Mifflin, 1940.)

Foa, U. G. A facet approach to the prediction of communalities. *Behavioral Science*, 1963, *8*, 220-226.

Fox, R. Balance and the problem of purpose in education. *Association for Supervision and Curriculum Development Yearbook*, 1961, 49-65.

Freud, A. *The ego and mechanisms of defense*. New York: International University Press, 1946.

Fromm, E. *Man for himself: An inquiry into the psychology of ethics*. New York: Rinehart, 1947.

Gardner, B. B., & Moore, D. G. *Human relations in industry*. Homewood, Ill.: Richard D. Irwin, 1952.

Getzels, J. W. Administration as a social process. In A. W. Halpin (Ed.), *Administrative theory in education*. Chicago: Midwest Administration Center, University of Chicago, 1958.

Gibb, C. A. Leadership. In G. Lindzey (Ed.), *Handbook of social psychology*. Cambridge, Mass.: Addison-Wesley, 1954.

Gladstone, A. The possibility of predicting reactions to international events. *Journal of Social Issues*, 1955, *11*, 21-28.

Goldstein, K. *Human nature in the light of psychopathology*. Cambridge, Mass.: Harvard University Press, 1940.

Gordon, J. W. Values in the classroom. *The National Elementary Principal*, 1962, *42*, 30-34.

Graff, O. *Better teaching in school administration*. Nashville, Tenn.: Southern States Cooperative Program in Educational Administration, George Peabody College, 1955.

Graff, O., & Kimbrough, R. What we have learned about selection. *Phi Delta Kappan*, 1956, *27*, 204-206.

Griffiths, D. E. *Human relations in school administration*. New York: Appleton-Century-Crofts, 1956.

Griffiths, D. E. *Administrative theory*. New York: Appleton-Century-Crofts, 1959.

Grobman, H. G., & Hines, V. A. What makes a good principal? *Bulletin of the National Association of Secondary School Principals*, 1956, *40*, 5-16.

Guba, E. G., & Bidwell, C. E. *Administrative relationships: Teacher effectiveness, teacher satisfaction, and administrative behavior; a study of the school as a social institution*. Chicago: Midwest Administration Center, University of Chicago, 1957.

Gulick, L. H., & Urwick, L. (Eds.). *Papers on the science of administration*. New York: Institute of Public Administration, Columbia University, 1937.

Guttman, L. Scale analysis. In S. Stouffer, *et al.*, *Measurement and prediction*. Princeton, N.J.: Princeton University Press, 1950.

Guttman, L. An outline of some new methodology for social research. *Public Opinion Quarterly*, 1954, *18*, 395-404.

Guttman, L. A structural theory for intergroup beliefs and attitudes. *American Sociology Review*, 1959, *24*, 318-328.

Haeberle, A. W. Friendship as an aspect of interpersonal relations. *Dissertation Abstracts*, 1959, *19*, 3353-3354.

Haire, M. (Ed.). *Modern organization theory: A symposium*. New York: John Wiley, 1959.

Hall, R., & McIntyre, K. The student personnel program. In R. Campbell & R. Gregg (Eds.), *Administrative behavior in education*. New York: Harper & Row, 1957.

Halpin, A. W. *The leadership behavior of school superintendents: The perceptions and expectations of board members, staff members, and superintendents*. Columbus, Ohio: College of Education, Ohio State University, 1956.

Halpin, A. W. *Administrative theory in education*. Chicago: Midwest Administration Center, University of Chicago, 1958.

Halpin, A. W., & Winer, B. J. A factorial description of the leader behavior descriptions. In R. M. Stogdill & A. E. Coons (Eds.), *Leader behavior: Its description and measurement*. Columbus, Ohio: Ohio State University, 1957.

Hansen, M., Hurwitz, W., & Madow, W. *Survey sample methods and theory*. Vol. 1. New York: John Wiley, 1953.

Harrell, T. W. Reliability and intercorrelation for thirteen leadership criteria. In *Perception of leadership in small groups*. Stanford, Calif.: Stanford University, 1964.

Haythorn, W. The influence of individual members on the characteristics of small groups. *Journal of Abnormal Social Psychology*, 1953, *48*, 276-284.

Hemphill, J. K. Why people attempt to lead. In L. Petrullo & B. M. Bass (Eds.), *Leadership and interpersonal behavior*. New York: Holt, Rinehart and Winston, 1961.

Hemphill, J. K., & Griffiths, D. E. *Administrative performance and personality: A study of the principal in a simulated elementary school.* New York: Bureau of Publications, Teachers College, Columbia University, 1962.

Hilkevitch, R. R. Social interaction processes. *Psychological Reports,* 1960, *7,* 195-201.

Hills, R. J. A new concept of staff relations. *Administrator's Notebook.* Chicago: Midwest Administration Center, University of Chicago, March, 1964.

Hines, V. Good principal—Effective leader. *Overview,* 1961, *2,* 31-32.

Hollander, E. P. Emergent leadership and social influence. In L. Petrullo & B. M. Bass (Eds.), *Leadership and interpersonal behavior.* New York: Holt, Rinehart and Winston, 1961.

Hollingshead, A. B. *Elmtown's youth.* New York: John Wiley, 1949.

Hollingshead, A. B., & Redlich, F. C. Social stratification and psychiatric disorders. *American Sociological Review,* 1953, *18,* 163-169.

Howarth, E. Extroversion and dream symbolism: An empirical study. *Psychological Reports,* 1962, *10,* 211-214.

Humphreys, L. The organization of human abilities. *American Psychologist,* 1962, *17,* 475-483.

Hyman, H. *Survey design and analysis.* Glencoe, Ill.: Free Press, 1955.

James, W. *Principles of psychology* (2 vols.). New York: Henry Holt, 1890.

Jung, C. G. *Psychological types.* London: Routledge & Kegan Paul, 1923.

Jung, C. G. Two essays on analytical psychology. *Collected works.* Vol. 7. New York: Pantheon, 1953.

Kellogg Foundation & University of Tennessee. *Characteristics of school administrators.* Knoxville, Tenn.: University of Tennessee, 1956.

Kimbrough, R. B. The behavioral characteristics of effective educational administrators. *Educational Administration Supervisor,* 1959, *45,* 337-348.

Kluckhohn, F. Values and value orientations in the theory of action. In T. Parsons & E. Shils (Eds.), *Toward a general theory of action.* Cambridge, Mass.: Harvard University Press, 1951.

Koch, H. L. The relation of "primary mental abilities" in five- and six-year olds to sex of child and characteristics of sibling. *Child Development,* 1954, *25,* 209-223.

Kriesberg, L. Economic rank and behavior. *Secondary Problems,* 1963, *4,* 334-352.

Laney, A. R. *Occupational implications of the Jungian personality functions-types as identified by the Briggs-Myers Type Indicator.* Unpublished master's thesis, George Washington University, 1949.

Lazarsfeld, P. F. Recent developments in latent structure analysis. *Sociometry,* 1956, *18,* 647-659.

Lazarsfeld, P. F., & Barton, A. H. Qualitative measurement in the social sciences. In D. Lerner & H. Lasswell (Eds.), *The policy sciences*. Stanford, Calif.: Stanford University Press, 1951.

Leary, T. F. *Interpersonal diagnosis of personality*. New York: Ronald Press, 1957.

Levinson, D. J. Role, personality, and social structure in the organizational setting. *Journal of Abnormal Social Psychology*, 1959, 58, 170-180.

Lewin, R., Lippitt, R., & White, R. K. Patterns of aggressive behavior in experimentally created climates. *Journal of Social Psychology*, 1939, 10, 271-279.

Lindquist, E. F. *Statistical analysis in educational research*. Boston: Houghton Mifflin, 1940.

Lipset, S. M., Lazarsfeld, P. F., Barton, A. H., & Linz, J. The psychology of voting. An analysis of political behavior. In G. Lindzey (Ed.), *Handbook of social psychology*. Cambridge, Mass.: Addison-Wesley, 1954.

Lord, F. M. *Multimodel score distributions on the Myers-Briggs Type Indicator—I* (Res. Memo. 58-8). Princeton, N.J.: Educational Testing Service, 1958.

Maccoby, E., & Rau, L. *Differential cognitive abilities*. Stanford, Calif.: Stanford University, 1962.

MacKinnon, D. W. The nature and nurture of creative talent. *American Psychologist*, 1962, 17, 484-495.

Madow, W. B. Personal communication, March, 1961.

Mann, H. *Lecture on education*. Boston: Marsh, Capen & Lyon, 1840.

March, J. G., & Simon, H. A. *Organizations*. New York: John Wiley, 1958.

Margenau, H. The scientific basis of value theory. In A. H. Maslow (Ed.), *New knowledge in human values*. New York: Harper & Row, 1959.

Maslow, A. H. (Ed.). *New knowledge in human values*. New York: Harper & Row, 1959.

May, R. R. *Existence*. New York: Basic Books, 1959.

McIntyre, K. *Recruiting and selecting leaders for education*. Austin, Texas: Southwest School Administration Center, University of Texas, 1955.

McKenna, D. Toward a theory in interpersonal relationships in the administration of higher education. *Journal of Education Research*, 1960, 54, 133-136.

Mead, G. *The Philosophy of the act*. Chicago: University of Chicago Press, 1938.

Mead, M. *The school in American culture*. Cambridge, Mass.: Harvard University Press, 1951.

Merton, R. K. Bureaucratic structure and personality. *Social Forces*, 1940, 17, 560-568. (Reprinted in N. J. Smelser & W. T. Smelser [Eds.], *Personality and social systems*. New York: John Wiley, 1963.)

Miller, V. Inner-direction and the decision maker. *School Executive*, 1959, 79, 27-29.

Miller, D. R., & Swanson, G. E. *The changing American parent*. New York: John Wiley, 1958.

Monroe, R. *Schools of psychoanalytic thought*. New York: Holt, Rinehart and Winston, 1955.

Moreno, J. *Who shall survive?* New York: Neuroses and Mental Disease Publishing Co., 1932.

Mort, P. R., et. al. *The growing edge: An instrument for measuring the adaptability of school systems*. New York: Metropolitan School Study Council, 1953.

Mort, P. R., & Ross, D. H. *Principles of school administration: A synthesis of basic concepts*. New York: McGraw-Hill, 1957.

Mussen, P. H., & Conger, J. J. *Child development and personality*. New York: Harper & Row, 1956.

Myers, I. B. *Manual (1962), The Myers-Briggs Type Indicator*. Princeton, N.J.: Educational Testing Service, 1962.

National Society for the Study of Education *Fifty-third yearbook. Part 1. Citizen cooperation for better public schools*. Chicago: University of Chicago, 1954.

Neagley, R. L. *CPEA reports to the profession on recruitment and selection of school administrators: A progress report*. New York: Teachers College, Columbia University, 1953.

Newell, C. A. Selection for leadership. *Educational Leadership*, 1962, 20, 179-181.

Newsome, G., & Gentry, H. Values and educational decisions. *The National Elementary Principal*, 1962, 42, 24-29.

North, C. C. & Hatt, R. K. The NORC scales. In A. J. Reiss, Jr., D. D. Duncan, R. K. Hatt & C. C. North, *Occupations and social stress*. Glencoe, Ill.: The Free Press, 1961.

Numberg, H. *Principles of psychoanalysis: Their application to the neuroses*. New York: International University Press, 1955.

Obradovic, S. *Interpersonal factors in the supervisor-teacher relationship*. Unpublished doctoral dissertation, University of California, Berkeley, 1962.

Parsons, T. *The social system*. Glencoe, Ill.: Free Press, 1951.

Petrullo, L., & Bass, B. M. (Eds.). *Leadership and interpersonal behavior*. New York: Holt, Rinehart and Winston, 1961.

Pettigrew, T. F. Social psychology and desegregation research. *American Psychologist*, 1961, 16, 105-112.

Platz, M. H. *Memorandum on competency pattern for school administration studies*. San Diego, Calif.: San Diego State College, 1960. Mimeographed.

Prince, R. Individual values and administrative effectiveness. *Administrator's Notebook*. Chicago: Midwest Administration Center, University of Chicago, December, 1957.

Pylinger, E., & Grace, W. *Emotional adjustment: A key to good citizenship*. Detroit: Wayne University Press, 1953.

Rapaport, D. The structure of psychoanalytic theory: A systematizing attempt. In S. Koch (Ed.), *Psychology: A study of a science* (Vol. 3). New York: McGraw-Hill, 1959.

Redl, F. Group emotion and leadership. *Psychiatry*, 1942, 5, 573-596. (Reprinted in A. P. Hare, E. F. Borgotta, & R. F. Bales [Eds.], *Small groups*. New York: Knopf, 1955.)

Reich, W. *The concept of space* (V. R. Carfagno, Translator). New York: Farrar, Straus & Giroux, 1958.

Reich, W. *The function of the orgasm*. New York: Farrar, Straus, Giroux, 1973.

Roberts, C. S. Ordinal position and its relationship to some aspects of personality. *Journal of Genetic Psychology*, 1938, 53, 173-213.

Roby, T. B. The executive function in small groups. In L. Petrullo & B. M. Bass (Eds.), *Leadership and interpersonal behavior*. New York: Holt, Rinehart and Winston, 1961.

Roethlisberger, F. L., & Dickson, W. J. *Management and the worker*. Cambridge, Mass.: Harvard University Press, 1939.

Roff, M. E. A study of combat leadership in the Air Force by use of a rating scale: Group differences. *Journal of Psychology*, 1950, 30, 229-239.

Rozenman, S. *Changes in interpersonal relations in the course of nondirective counseling*. Unpublished doctoral dissertation, Harvard University, 1953.

Rosenzweig, S. Investigating and appraising personality. In T. G. Andrews (Ed.), *Methods of psychology*. New York: John Wiley, 1948.

Ross, J. *Progress report on the college student characteristics study: June, 1961* (Res. Memo. 61-11). Princeton, N.J.: Educational Testing Service, 1961.

Sampson, E. An experiment on active and passive resistance to social power. *Dissertation Abstracts*, 1961, 21, 2393.

Saunders, D. R. *Evidence bearing on use of the Myers-Briggs Type Indicator to select persons for advanced religious training: A preliminary report* (Res. Bull. 57-8). Princeton, N.J.: Educational Testing Service, 1957.

Saunders, D. R. *Evidence bearing on the existence of a rational correspondence between the personality typologies of Spranger and Jung* (Res. Bull. 60-6). Princeton, N.J.: Educational Testing Service, 1960.

Schachter, S. *The psychology of affiliation*. Stanford, Calif.: Stanford University Press, 1959.

Scheidlinger, S. *Psychoanalysis and group behavior*. New York: Norton, 1957.

Schutz, W. Theory and measurement of content analysis. (Doctoral dissertation, University of California, Los Angeles, 1950).

Schutz, W. Reliability, ambiguity and content analysis. *Psychological Review*, 1952.

Schutz, W. What makes groups productive? *Human Relations*, 1955, *8*, 429-465.

Schutz, W. The interpersonal underworld. *Harvard Business Review*, 1958, *36*, 123-135.

Schutz, W. On categorizing qualitative data. *Public Opinion Quarterly*, 1959, *22*, 503-515.

Schutz, W. *An outline of research design*. Unpublished manuscript, 1961.(a)

Schutz, W. The ego, FIRO theory and the leader as completer. In L. Petrullo & B. M. Bass (Eds.), *Leadership and interpersonal behavior*. New York: Holt, Rinehart and Winston, 1961.(b)

Schutz, W. *Procedures for identifying persons with potential for public school administrative positions*. Berkeley, Calif.: University of California, 1961.(c)

Schutz, W. *The interpersonal underworld (FIRO)*. Palo Alto, Calif.: Science and Behavior Books, 1966. (Originally published, 1958.)

Schutz, W. *Here comes everybody*. New York: Harper & Row, 1973.

Schutz, W. *Elements of Encounter*. New York: Bantam, 1975.

Schutz, W. *EVY: An odyssey into bodymind*. New York: Harper & Row, 1976.(a)

Schutz, W. The FIRO administrator: theory, criteria, and measurement of effectiveness. *Group & Organization Studies: The International Journal for Group Facilitators*, 1976, *1* (2), 154-176.(b)

Schutz, W. *Profound simplicity*. New York: Bantam, in press.

Schutz, W., & Krasnow, E. An IBM 704-707 program for Guttman scaling. *Behavioral Science*, 1964, *9*, 87.

Schwartz, S. Review of research and empirical applications of FIRO theory. In W. Schutz, *FIRO scales manual* (revised). Palo Alto, Calif.: Consulting Psychologists Press, 1976.

Scott, W. International ideology and interpersonal ideology. *Public Opinion Quarterly*, 1960, *24*, 419-435.

Sears, P. S. Doll play aggression in normal young children: Influence of sex, age, sibling status, father's absence. *Psychological Monographs*, 1951, *65*, No. 6 (whole No. 323).

Sears, R. R. Ordinal position in the family as a psychological variable. *American Sociological Review*, 1950, *15*, 397-401.

Sears, R. R., Maccoby, E. E., & Levin, H. *Patterns of child rearing*. Evanston, Ill.: Row, Peterson, 1957.

Semrad, E. V., & Arsenian, J. The use of group processes in teaching group dynamics. *American Journal of Psychiatry*, 1951, *108*, 358-363.

Sharp, G. Principal as a professional leader. *The National Elementary Principal*, 1962, *42*, 61-63.

Shartle, C. L. *Occupational information.* Englewood Cliffs, N.J.: Prentice-Hall, 1952.

Shartle, C. L. Leadership and organizational behavior. In L. Petrullo & B. M. Bass (Eds.), *Leadership and interpersonal behavior.* New York: Holt, Rinehart and Winston, 1961.

Shaw, M. E. A comparison of two types of leadership in various communication nets. *Journal of Abnormal Social Psychology*, 1955, *50*, 127-134.

Simon, H. A behavioral model of rational choice. *Quarterly Journal of Economics*, 1955, *69*, 99-118.

Slater, P. *Psychological factors in role specialization.* Unpublished doctoral dissertation, Harvard University, 1955.

Sorokin, P. A. *Social and cultural dynamics.* New York: American Books, 1937.

Stewart, L. *Birth order and political genius: I. Presidents of the United States.* Paper read to California Psychological Association, December, 1961.

Stiles, L. J. *The teacher's role in American society.* New York: Harper & Row, 1957.

Stogdill, R. M. Personal factors associated with leadership: A survey of the literature. *Journal of Psychology*, 1948, *25*, 35-71.

Stogdill, R. M., & Shartle, C. L. Methods for determining patterns of leadership in relation to organization structure and objectives. *Journal of Applied Psychology*, 1948, *32*, 286-291.

Stoke, S. M. An inquiry into the concept of identification. *Journal of Genetic Psychology*, 1950, *76*, 163-189.

Stricker, L., & Ross, J. *The item content and some correlates of a Jungian personality inventory* (Res. Bull. 62-6). Princeton, N.J.: Educational Testing Service, 1963.

Suzuki, D. T. Human values in Zen. In A. H. Maslow (Ed.), *New knowledge in human values.* New York: Harper & Row, 1959.

Symonds, P. M. *The dynamics of human adjustment.* New York: Appleton-Century, 1946.

Taylor, F. W. *Scientific management.* New York: Harper & Row, 1947.

Taylor, M., Crook, R., & Dropkin, S. Assessing emerging leadership behavior in small discussion groups. *Journal of Educational Psychology*, 1961, *2*, 12-18.

Terman, L. M. *Concept mastery test.* New York: Psychological Corp., 1956.

Tillich, P. Is a science of human values possible? In A. H. Maslow (Ed.), *New knowledge in human values.* New York: Harper & Row, 1959.

Tryon, P. C. Communality of a variable: Formulation by cluster analysis. *Psychometrika*, 1957, *22*, 241-260.

Tyler, F. B., Rafferty, J. E., & Tyler, B. B. Relationships among motivations of parents and their children. *Journal of Genetic Psychology*, 1962, *101*, 69-81.

216   *Leaders of Schools*

U.S. Bureau of the Census. *U.S. Census of Population: 1960*. Washington, D.C.: U.S. Government Printing Office, 1961.

von Fange, E. A. Implications for school administration of the personality structure of educational personnel. Unpublished doctoral dissertation, University of Alberta, 1961.

Waelder, R. The problem of the genesis of psychical conflicts in earliest infancy. *International Journal of Psychoanalysis*, 1937, *18*, 406-473.

Warner, W. L. *Social class in America*. (Rev. ed.) New York: Harper & Row, 1960.

Waxler, N. *Defense mechanisms and interpersonal behavior*. Unpublished doctoral dissertation, Harvard University, 1960.

Weisskopf, W. Existence and values. In A. H. Maslow (Ed.), *New knowledge in human values*. New York: Harper & Row, 1959.

Weldy, G. R. Teachers evaluate their principal. *National Association of Secondary School Principals Bulletin*, 1961, *45*, 145-150.

Wetzler, W. F. The marks of a successful school administrator. *American School Board Journal*, 1955, *131*, 42-43.

Willower, D. Values and educational administration. *Peabody Journal of Education*, 1961, *39*, 157-161.

Wirth, A. Values for educators. *Educational Leadership*, 1961, *18*, 493-496.